Appreciating Risk Management

Discover the Advantages of a Strategic Partnership

By Andrew S. (Andy) Martin, CLU, ChFC
and Todd Russell, CFP®, CLU, ChFC

ISBN: 9781710060737

All rights reserved. No part of this book may be reproduced or transmitted in any form or by any means, electronic or mechanical, including photocopying, recording, or by any information storage and retrieval system, without permission in writing from the copyright owners.

Table of Contents

Preface…..7

Introduction: Protecting Your Clients and Your Business…..13

Chapter 1: Are You Prepared for Disruption in Your Industry?.....23

There are some big changes coming…are you ready?

Chapter 2: Your Clients Need These Services!.....44

How not to put your clients' assets at risk

Chapter 3: Building a Fence Around Your Client…..59

Are you making it easier for your clients to leave?

Chapter 4: Staying in Your Own Lane…..80

Focusing on the Highest and Best Use of Your Time

Chapter 5: Focusing on Simplicity…..93

Simplifying your life by simplifying your business

Chapter 6: Leveraging Expertise…..107

Reaching out to your team of specialists

Chapter 7: Next Steps and Case Studies…..121

Where do we go from here?

Additional Resources…..153

About the Authors…..154

Disclosures…..159

The author is a registered representative of Lincoln Financial Securities. Securities and investment advisory services offered through Lincoln Financial Securities Corp., a broker/dealer (member SIPC) and a registered investment advisor.

The material here reflects the views of the author and not necessarily those of Lincoln Financial Securities or its affiliates. This material is intended for educational purposes only and should not be used as investment advice or recommendations.

This book highlights important industry regulations and concepts. Please review these resources and concepts and consult your tax, financial and legal professionals before implementing or making changes in a retirement plan.

Annuities are long-term retirement savings or income vehicles. There are fixed and variable annuities available; variable annuities are sold by prospectus. An investor should carefully consider the investment objectives, risks, charges, and expenses of the variable product and its underlying investment options carefully before investing. The prospectus contains this and other information about the variable product and its underlying investment options. Always read it carefully before investing.

All rights reserved. No part of this book may be used or reproduced in any manner whatsoever without written permission from **the Author** except as provided by the United States of America copyright law or in the case of brief quotations embodied in articles and reviews.

The scanning, uploading and distribution of this book via the Internet or via any other means without the permission of the publisher is illegal and punishable by law.

Please purchase only authorized electronic editions and do not participate in or encourage electronic piracy of copyrighted materials. Your support of the author's rights is sincerely appreciated.

Preface

With change comes opportunity

If you are a financial advisor or multi-line insurance professional, you've likely noticed some big changes taking place in the industry – with even more on the way. These not only affect how you work with your clients, but they can also impact the manner and the frequency regarding how you get paid.

Most advisors in the financial services field work towards building recurring revenue. Depending on your particular focus area, this may be done through the sale of insurance coverage (with regular premiums due), or by building up assets under management and earning an annual fee for your advice.

Unfortunately, though, transaction type services are going by the wayside. In addition, due in large part to regulatory changes, the commissions and fees charged by financial advisors (at least the ones that are human) are also waning. So, by going about "business as usual," many multi-line insurance and financial professionals may find that the amount of their paychecks will decrease over time.

Then what?

No Business is "Too Big" to Fail

Doing things the way they have always been done isn't necessarily a recipe for success in the financial services business. In fact, going this route could actually take you down a sure path to disaster.

Over time, even large and seemingly "unshrinkable" companies like Kodak, Blockbuster, Nokia, and IBM, have disappeared by not looking – or planning – ahead and adapting.

But with change can also come opportunity. So, it only makes sense to roll with the changes if you want to keep your business thriving over the long term. One of the most effective ways to do that is by offering valuable services that your clients need so they don't have to turn to your competition in order to get them.

This book is targeted to financial advisors, multi-line insurance agents, and professionals who specialize in providing employee benefits, and who are able to receive revenue from the sale of insurance.

While many advisors know that their clients need protection that tools like life insurance can provide, for one reason or another, you may be uncomfortable bringing up this topic with your customers.

Even though your clients know that you are highly qualified at what you do, it is possible that you're simply not comfortable discussing life insurance solutions, and in turn being perceived as an "insurance agent" (and less "professional") in the eyes of your customers.

Plus, if you don't make these types of coverage recommendations on a regular basis, you could also be leery about being asked questions that you're not able to answer. With that in mind, it is oftentimes easier not to bring up the subject at all. This, however, could lead to some unenticing results for you and your clients.

Is This Book for You?

If you know that your clients have gaps in their financial protection, but you just simply don't have the time or the resources to address these additional needs, this book can provide you with a solution…and it won't cost you additional time or money to implement.

We specialize in helping multi-line insurance professionals and financial advisors address the overall needs of their clients, which in turn can help to grow their businesses. We understand that many property and casualty agents are concerned about the "commoditization" of their businesses and are likely to see rates go down in the future.

These professionals also have to live with the pricing of competitors that regularly advertise "savings" if clients make a switch and go directly to them to purchase their coverage. This can be unnerving – especially as you work to maximize the potential value of your customers.

Similarly, the producer we identify as the financial advisor often markets themselves as a financial consultant or financial planner. Most who work in this niche are focused on gathering assets.

Oftentimes, these advisors come into the financial services industry as an insurance specialist, but eventually morph their business over to an investment-based practice because their clients need these services, too.

In many instances, it doesn't take long for financial advisors to find that providing investment-related services is much easier than selling protection-based offerings. Doing so also leads to faster pay days, as it can often take weeks (or even longer) for a life insurance application to work its way through underwriting – and even then, there is no guarantee that the applicant will be approved.

This isn't the case when offering investments or most other types of insurance protection such as auto and homeowners. Plus, "transactional" sales like selling shares of stock or mutual funds can provide a much faster time frame between prospect and paycheck.

On top of that, life insurance in particular can be a touchy subject for investment advisors as well as multi-line insurance agents to bring up with clients. Asking in-depth questions about various medical issues, family health history, and medications being taken can be downright uncomfortable – particularly for advisors who are used to dealing more with rates of return and P/E ratios or the insurable value of one's home and auto.

Given the plethora of personal questions that must be asked to clients, along with the lengthy underwriting process, many financial advisors and multi-line insurance agents alike have a distaste for solving life insurance protection needs.

Even so, however, the need for protection still exists for clients – and avoiding the topic of life insurance with customers could not only leave their loved ones in a state of future financial hardship, but may even lead to legal action against advisors who had the ability and the opportunity to address the issue, but didn't.

The big question is, then, are you leaving big holes in your clients' financial plans and in turn, adding to the risk exposure of your business?

If so — and many advisors are — it could be advantageous to partner with a specialist in this area. In fact, there are many ways that a risk management or insurance specialist can help advisors. For instance, collaborating with an accomplished resource can allow you to do more holistic planning for clients, without having to become laser focused on a new line of business, or even be affiliated with life insurance coverage providers.

A life insurance specialist can also work with advisors to look forward and more accurately forecast revenue over the long-term — even given future pay-related regulations and regulatory trends.

As you will learn in this book, the number of truly qualified people who are available to help your clients with their life insurance protection needs has diminished. So, even if you've been searching for help in this area, you may not know where to turn.

The good news is that there are still potential solutions for getting your clients the services that they need…and they can be found right here!

Introduction: Protecting Your Clients and Your Business

As a financial advisor, multi-line insurance, or employee benefits professional, one of your top priorities is to help your clients grow their assets or their business, while at the same time protecting what they have built – particularly as they inch ever closer to retirement.

It is possible that many of your clients' financial protection needs could be solved using insurance-based solutions. Unfortunately, though, risk management planning is oftentimes avoided, not just by clients, but also by the advisors who serve them – even though assets could be significantly diminished by taxes or inadequate transfer strategies without it.

There are a couple of reasons why risk management through insurance solutions may be bypassed by even the most sophisticated advisors. One is because it can be a somewhat uncomfortable topic to discuss. For instance, few people relish the idea of thinking about how things will be when they are gone.

Similarly, bringing up the concept of planning for premature death or the financial ravages of an extended health care incident can also make some advisors uneasy. In this case, shifting gears from a discussion about investment returns and retirement income strategies to one about pre-existing conditions and other types of health issues is uncharted territory for many financial professionals.

In addition, many of today's insurance policies can have a lot of "moving parts," making them difficult for clients to fully understand, and challenging for even the best multi-line insurance, employee benefits specialist, or financial professionals to explain.

On top of that, even if you've determined that a client needs insurance coverage, the application and underwriting process can be quite tedious – sometimes taking up to several weeks (or more) when factoring in a medical exam and / or pertinent information that is required from the applicant's health care professional(s).

For a financial or insurance advisor who doesn't specialize in life coverage, there is also the risk of submitting paperwork or making other common mistakes that could in turn require you to go back to the client – possibly even numerous times – for gathering additional information. Doing so, though, adds significant stress to you and your staff, and could even wreak havoc on your credibility as a competent professional.

Likewise, if incorrect premium rates are quoted, such as the lower cost for a "preferred" applicant when in fact the client is only accepted at the "standard" or "sub-standard" rate, it may leave the client feeling like they've been a victim of "bait and switch."

Adding more fuel to the fire can make matters worse if the insurance company does not accept the client at all for the policy. In fact, this scenario could even put your relationship with the client at risk going forward.

So, how can you ensure that your clients are being well-served in all areas of financial planning and protection, but without you having to become an expert in insurance or be perceived as a salesy insurance "peddler?"

The good news is that you don't have to, because you have options.

How to Keep Your Clients Protected

Today, specialization is the name of the game if you want to attract and retain your ideal clients. With that in mind, though, if you don't work with particular financial vehicles on a regular basis, it can be stressful to approach clients with such vehicles as a solution for them...even if it's the appropriate recommendation.

If your focus lies primarily in gathering assets under management, wealth management, multi-line coverage, retirement planning, or employee benefits, it is possible that you've shied away from offering traditional insurance solutions to your clients.

A survey by Saybrus Partners found that financial advisors largely avoid discussing life insurance with their clients because "the subject is unsexy, time-consuming, and / or too complicated."

The study went on to say that nearly half of those advisors who were polled stated that life insurance was a "distraction from their regular practice", with another 17% declaring that it was just "too complicated," which could cause advisors to make mistakes when presenting and applying for such coverage.[1]

Regardless of one's feelings about insurance solutions, though, it doesn't mean that clients should go without them. In fact, if there is a need for this type of financial protection, you could actually be doing your clients a disservice by not offering it.

So, what happens if you're not well-versed in insurance concepts, but you uncover the need for it, and it provides the ideal solution for clients' needs?

That's when it may be time to consider adding a risk management specialist to your team.

Why Working with a Risk Management Specialist is a Win-Win

Even if the need for an insurance based solution is clear, and you know that this type of specialist can offer your clients the right option(s) for their protection needs, should you be directly involved in the process? Or alternatively, would your clients be better served by referring them to a specialist who can quickly and easily answer their questions and concerns?

There are multiple benefits for both advisors and their clients when turning to a risk management specialist. First and foremost, it's the right thing to do in that it allows client needs to be specifically addressed – and questions to be answered - without you having to learn all the intricacies of these highly complex products.

In addition, by going out into the marketplace, a specialist can compare various options, and ensure that the coverage, pricing, and underwriting requirements all line up with the needs and goals of your client.

As an example, one common situation which can increase the likelihood of a bad experience is not asking medical questions prior to selecting the carrier in which to apply. We had a relatively healthy client who was in need of term coverage. The only "blip" on their file was a family history of cardiovascular disease, resulting in their father's death in his mid-40's.

Based on the client's personal health merit, they would have received the best class rates. However, due to family history, many companies limited him to the 3rd best class, resulting in an excessive premium charge.

Without a specialist involved, many clients would be stuck with paying the higher premium rate. However, knowing the market and the carrier guidelines, we were able to secure the second best rate class for the client. This, in turn, saved him a great deal of money over time. It also helped to further solidify the relationship with the client, as he felt comfortable knowing that we had his best interest in mind.

Most financial advisors and insurance generalists work hard to develop strategies that are right for their clients. This includes offering various "tools" that fit within the parameters of the client's short- and long-term objectives.

Just like a general medical practitioner maintains his or her patients - but refers them to a specialist when more in-depth care is required - the same concept holds true with financial and risk management planning.

In this case, an experienced insurance professional can provide access to numerous options, and in turn, can match the best type and amount of coverage for clients' needs. Just some of the additional benefits can include:

- Educating the client on how the process works, and on what to anticipate
- Communicating with clients and gathering any additional information that may be needed from the insurance carrier
- Providing the client with realistic premium quotes
- Managing realistic expectations with regard to acceptance or rejection for coverage

Working with a sophisticated insurance specialist as a member of your team can also result in additional revenue for your firm, but without you personally having to expend time communicating with underwriters, submitting all the proper paperwork, and even getting a "second opinion" from other insurance carriers if your client is rejected for coverage.

Many people find themselves looking at multiple spreadsheets that can get so confusing that they end up wasting time that could be better invested in their area of core competency.

Some end up even more stressed with too many options and in turn, can fall victim to "analysis paralysis" which can slow or even damage the process of protecting their clients.

All of this is done with you still being kept in the loop, too, but without taking you away from the services that you provide best. If you are properly licensed to receive insurance commissions, we incorporate a revenue-share on the client's application for coverage. So that way, you can share in the compensation, and the ongoing trailing revenue as well.

Today's life insurance solutions can be far more complex than they were even just a decade ago. But that doesn't negate clients' need for this coverage. In fact, more options and benefits have only made this business more complex - and made the need for specialization grow.

Want to find out more about how you can uncover and protect your clients' needs, and continue to earn revenue from insurance based solutions, but without adding more work for yourself?

If so, turn the page and let's get started!

Sources

1. Many Advisors Don't 'Get' Life Insurance. Financial Advisor magazine. August 5, 2013. https://www.fa-mag.com/news/many-advisors-don-t--get--life-insurance-15059.html

Chapter 1: Are You Prepared for Disruption in Your Industry?

There are some big changes coming...are you ready?

It has often been said that "the only constant in life is change." This is certainly the case in the financial services industry. Although it is necessary for any company or business to evolve, changes like new industry regulations have been unsettling to some, while at the same time viewed as an opportunity by others.

Some of these changes could eventually force advisors to either add additional offerings that clients need, or to radically change their whole business model. For instance, technology is in the process of disrupting the "traditional" insurance and financial services business. The price driven, low advice based, low relationship driven sale is in jeopardy to new direct-to-consumer firms that can provide better pricing while also appearing to give more choice.

With that in mind, advisors need to have systems in place that will improve client engagement and

retention, and that will also provide much-needed revenue sources to help with maximizing profitability per client.

One way to accomplish this is by adding additional risk management tools that most clients already need. Unfortunately, though, most firms are hesitant to start a cross-marketing strategy – even though the upside to doing this can be significant.

Why is that?

Depending on whether you view industry changes as friend or foe can have a significant impact on the future of your revenue, and ultimately on your firm. Moving forward successfully – and even expanding the breadth of your business – can take time and effort. That is, unless you focus on what you do best, and delegate the rest.

Being Mindful of Key Trends

Let's face it. The financial services market is changing. What was once a highly personal "sit at the kitchen table with clients" type of business is now being disrupted by a multitude of innovations, modifications, and regulations.

In fact, according to Morningstar, "Investment advisors are being pushed out of the investment market." With the advent of packaged investment products – and their enthusiastic embrace by fund companies and consumers alike – today the industry's landscape is far different than it was even just a few years ago.[1]

In light of such changes, some firms will adapt and survive. Others, however, will not.

Regulations from both state and federal government – as well as from the self-regulatory officials – have always had the ability to change how the financial services industry is run. So, not being properly prepared can come back to bite you.

All regulators discuss the importance of "knowing your customer." If you take time to get a complete fact finder, that covers all aspects of wealth management. It can help you to do a better job of serving them.

In the financial services industry, changes often occur that require advisors to adapt. For some advisors, this can be unsettling. But for others, heightened regulations in the industry can provide an opportunity to get better.

This can help you do a better job of uncovering needs clients may not even know they have. It also is impressive if you can show a supervisor how thoroughly you know your customers because of the information documented in a comprehensive fact finder.

It's not possible to predict what will happen with legislation going forward. But, understanding that change will happen – and deciding how to respond to it – can help you plan strategically in order to make change more "friendly". Those who do not plan for this change, though, may be left behind as others move on.

Entire businesses are being impacted by new regulations, which could dramatically affect the way that financial professionals conduct business in the future. In some cases, veteran advisors may even become frustrated to the point of leaving the financial services industry by way of retirement or making a career change.

Others are changing what they offer to their clients due in large part to what they feel is "excessive" compliance issues. In many ways, then, heightened regulation and compliance can even lend to not addressing risk management needs at all.

But is this really in the best interest of clients?

It's not if you want to ensure that their financial plan is complete and that their assets – and their loved ones – are protected from a long list of potential risks. Nor is it the best way to address your own business needs going forward.

In an environment of heightened regulation and compliance, many advisors actually avoid having conversations with their clients about risk management. This is often because of the time-consuming nature of these products from application to approval, and from application to policy placement.

Another big reason for starting a conversation about risk management with clients is because if an advisor doesn't address these issues, they could be failing to properly serve their client's needs. So, avoiding the issue altogether can sometimes seem like the "safer" road to take, but we have to ask ourselves if it is the best road to take.

Advisors are also leery about bringing up a topic where they may not know all the answers. In this case, rather than appearing unprofessional or unprepared in the eyes of the client, it is often much more comfortable to let this particular issue slide. But this runs the risk of clients that trust their advisor explicitly not being aware of potential holes in their plan.

One thing is for sure, though. Industry regulators want to believe that the best interests of the consumer are being protected. Exactly how they have defined that over the years has been somewhat of a mystery.

So, what are some of the key trends that are facing the industry today?

One is the possibility of a slowing demand for property and casualty coverage offerings, as well as for "costly" wealth management advice. For instance, there are two primary forces causing disruption in the multi-line niche.

One is the reduction in claims, due in large part to the emerging safety technology in today's vehicles, such as back-up cameras and blind spot indicators. This "safer" driving technology will in turn have an impact on the pricing of auto coverage, which will likely cause a related decrease in agents' commissions.

Likewise, the concept of "shared autos" – particularly in large and mid-sized cities – can further reduce the need for individual auto coverage, and in turn, in the commission income of multi-line agents and brokers.

The same types of trends are making their way into the homeowner's market, too. In this case, many consumers who once owned vacation or second homes are now turning towards "interval" ownership, which eliminates the need to insure these properties (at least by the individual consumer).

Further, as technology becomes more embedded in our everyday lives, there comes another factor that is impacting multi-line firms. This has to do with the direct to consumer companies – many of which advertise how much individuals can save on their coverage. These savings are based in large part on these companies' low overhead, as well as their work with carriers that are specifically designed to minimize cost by not compensating the investment advisor or the insurance agent.

Many consumers – including high net worth investors – are also changing the way they look at, and pay for, financial planning advice. Ironically, until roughly 20 years ago, most insurance advisors earned the majority of their income from the sale of insurance products. Today, however, many insurance professionals have adapted to where they receive the bulk of their income from investments.

> *Because of this, wealth advisors are facing pay cuts, too. Often referred to as "fee compression," the advent of robo advisors and low-cost mutual funds have increasingly led consumers to view portfolio advice as a commodity, and in turn to shop for lower-priced financial advice.*

Even large advisory platforms are jumping into the price cut game. For instance, in 2018, LPL Financial – the #1 independent broker-dealer - announced that it was lowering pricing across both its corporate and advisory platforms.[2]

The firm added a no-transaction-fee mutual fund network to its Strategic Wealth Management platform. It also reduced pricing on its Strategic Asset Management advisory platform. In addition, as of mid-2019, LPL started cutting ETF (Exchange Traded Fund) ticket charges by nearly half for three major fund families.[3]

One reason for these changes at LPL is for the purpose of holding on to assets under management. But the Department of Labor's fiduciary rule also played a key role in the decision to make these moves.[4]

High net worth individuals are in high demand by private wealth managers. The more money someone has, though, the more work it can take for maintaining and preserving assets. So, it can be difficult for advisors to spend more time on clients' needs while at the same time earning less.

For the most part, advisors don't want to charge so much that they drive away business. On the other hand, charging too little can make wealth management services appear less valuable. The average fee for a professional advisor's services runs in the neighborhood of 1%, depending on the amount of assets under management. But online advisors have shown that a reasonable fee for money management is only about 0.25% to 0.30% of assets – and that many wealth managers nowadays need to justify why clients should pay more.[5]

How will the movement away from commission-based sales and higher asset management fees impact your bottom line?

Yet another disruption in the industry has to do with large retailers like Walmart and Amazon dipping their toe into the risk management and financial services niche. These mammoth companies are now providing everything from banking to investments and insurance, either as direct providers of coverage or as supporters of other entities that offer protection.

In a recent study regarding Amazon and other FinTech entities, Insurance Innovators research firm stated that, "Industry insiders are in no doubt that these firms are preparing to wreak 'Uber-style' disruption on insurance." The most successful digital platforms are either expected to offer their own insurance or provide access to third-party providers.[6]

In fact, it is estimated that Amazon is the platform that is most likely to cause widespread disruption to Europe's general insurance market over the next five years. So, it's possible that a similar scenario may also take place soon in the United States.[7]

The digital marketplace is also changing the financial services and insurance business. Today, consumers are literally bombarded with online messages and ads trying to lure customers in by comparing coverage and prices.

Even the simple act of searching for insurance quotes online can lead to a barrage of pop up ads appearing on consumers' servers for months afterwards, "reminding" them how much they can save on their premiums. This can be dangerous for multi-line agents, and it could ultimately force many to remain in the price sensitive part of the market. Unfortunately, though, competing on price alone can be a never-ending battle.

Similarly, "stock pickers" are no longer needed today, as consumers can easily jump online and view real-time quotes, projections, and research reports. Investors can also opt for "baskets" of pre-selected stocks by way of the exchange traded fund. Going this route can save hours of research and analysis. But it also negates the need for professional investment advice, as consumers can purchase a whole host of financial vehicles with just the click of a mouse.

Additional financial services industry disruption comes from the rise of the robo-advisor, an online platform that produces automated risk management and investment "advice," based on various algorithms, without the need for any human intervention.

Even given all of these industry disruptions, such as lower premium cost, immediate stock price quotes, and the convenience of obtaining insurance protection online, there is at least some good news in that there are still consumers and businesses that prefer to work with a personal specialist in these areas.[8]

By engaging more with your customers, then, you'll have a much better chance of establishing, and maintaining ongoing relationships, even in the face of emerging digital technology. In fact, by blending technology with personal client engagement, you can become a trusted professional who can provide clients with advice on their financial needs and insurance protection.

Financial giant Vanguard maintains that "advisors should focus on client relationships, perhaps even including behavioral coaching and some more complex financial planning, but certainly advisors should have very little to do with traditional investment selection."[9]

Some advisors have already transitioned in both their own minds, as well as in the public's perception, from being investment or insurance professionals to being relationship managers.

So, if you are able to provide clients with advice, along with a team approach that consists of specialists in the various components of their overall plan, it is likely that you will retain clients for a longer period of time. You will also do a better job of overall planning for your clients, which can lead to additional business.

More Services Offered = Better Client Retention

On top of the many changes in the financial services industry today, there is also a great deal of competition in the marketplace. Take a look around you and see how many people – even within just a one-mile radius in some areas - are marketing themselves in a similar manner.

This being the case, how are you differentiating yourself from them? And what could you do to get your ideal clients to come to you – even if they have to pass several other advisors' offices in order to get to you?

Good customer retention isn't just something that's "nice to have." Rather, it is necessary for survival. In fact, in today's highly competitive marketplace, customer retention could be *the* most significant factor in the sustainability and profitability of your business.

A primary reason for this is because in the insurance industry, it can cost up to nine times as much to acquire a new customer than it does to retain a current one. There is also a very strong correlation between high customer retention rates and sustainable profit margins. So, if your agency suffers a high customer "churn" rate, your profits can be eaten up by the cost of replacing your lost customers.[10]

With that in mind, many forward-thinking firms understand just how important being successful in this market is to the future of their business. Your clients need these services regardless, so it's likely that they're going to obtain them from somewhere.

Why shouldn't that "somewhere" be you?

But, how can you dive into additional coverage alternatives - and enhance your customer retention - without having to branch out into uncharted territory and risk being asked questions you can't answer about offerings that you're not entirely familiar with?

The answer: By taking a TEAM approach.

Research shows (and our current experience would substantiate) that clients actually prefer a team approach. Using this method – which we refer to as an ensemble – clients can feel more secure, knowing that they have specialists to rely upon for even the most in-depth risk management needs. This could be one reason why solo practitioners secure less business than teams do.

Without access to the solutions your customers require, you run the risk of them picking up and going somewhere else to solve these needs. You also risk the possibility of clients gradually (or possibly even abruptly) moving all of their business elsewhere to firms that can assist them with the entire investment and risk management plan, all under one roof.

The Increasing Need to Offer More Comprehensive Solutions

Because life is ever-changing, the need for wealth management and protection can be a continuous moving target. Families add, and lose, members. Big events like weddings, the birth of children, opening a business, or retirement are anxiously awaited and are times when needs for additional planning are at a peak.

Also, many successful people spend their health building their wealth. Since their health can eventually decline, they may require more sophisticated planning to help them offset the financial ravages of an extended health care incident or replacing their income if they are not able to work.

These life-altering events can bring about new and expensive "liabilities" for clients, which in turn can create the need for additional planning. There is also a multitude of life changes that can require clients to add or update their insurance coverage, such as:

- Marriage or divorce
- Weddings
- Birth of a child or grandchild
- Purchase of a new home
- Job change or promotion
- Retirement
- Preparation for potential long-term care needs
- Need for future guaranteed income
- Asset transfer and wealth protection needs

Clients are most likely to need assistance when they face a life event. With that in mind, it is essential that multi-line agents and financial advisors have someone who can train their customer service representatives on how and where to look for opportunities.

It is also important to let clients know the breadth of services your firm offers. Otherwise, it is likely that you'll hear at least some of your clients say, "I went to the advisor down the street because I didn't know you did that."

Determining new or uncovered risks can be accomplished through regular communication or annual reviews with clients. While this is likely not your core competency, a risk management specialist can serve your clients with traditional needs analysis or reviews of their existing coverage.

How Can You Keep Your Business Thriving Without Adding More Hours to Your Workday?

Many of the most sophisticated firms understand the importance of maximizing revenue from existing clients.

According to the EY 2016 Property and Casualty Insurance Outlook, and research provided by LIMRA, multi-line firms need to be prepared for several market forces that could change the profitability of the business, and for some, the viability of their businesses going forward.

In today's environment of potentially losing income to fee compression, the costs of regulation and compliance, and direct competitors, it is critical to maximize opportunities to serve your existing client base.

If your business is currently producing a nice income for you, it is easy to become comfortable and complacent. After all, it is human nature to gravitate towards our comfort zones and to hope that the changes around us will be minimal. But as most people know, hope is not a strategy.

That is why most elite performers are continuously surveying the headwinds of the market and assessing their competition, at times even looking for ways to "reinvent" themselves in order to keep up with the changes, focus on emerging markets, and work towards experiencing explosive growth.

It's never easy to make a drastic move. Our goal in this book is to show you how you can seamlessly make incremental improvement and begin the journey towards offering your clients the holistic services they need.

And believe it or not, you can do so without having to expend more time or learn a whole new "language" of risk management terms and strategies!

Think about it like this. The Tennessee Titans would not likely put their kicker in the game in place of the team's quarterback. In fact, the kicker rarely sees more than just a few seconds of actual game time.

But when it comes down to making that game-winning field goal, it's nice to know that there's a specialist the team can rely on to get the job done. Then, when the scoreboard ticks down the last second, everyone celebrates the win as a team.

Sources

1. Morningstar. https://www.morningstar.com/blog/2018/07/12/invest-advisor.html
2. LPL Cust Pricing Across Corporate Hybrid RIA Platform. https://www.thinkadvisor.com/2018/04/26/lpl-cuts-pricing-across-corporate-hybrid-ria-platf/?slreturn=20190708104311
3. LPL isn't ruling out zero-fee ETFs in RIA push. Financial-planning.com/news/lpl-financial-cuts-transaction-charges-on-etfs
4. LPL Simplifies and Cuts Fees for Advisors. Financialadvisoriq.com/c/1789623/208993
5. How to Cut Financial Advisor Expenses. Investopedia. Investopedia.com/articles/personal-finance/071415/how-cut-financial-adisor-expenses.asp
6. Insurers rank Amazon as the world's most potentially disruptive platform. https://www.theactuary.com/news/2018/11/insurers-rank-amazon-as-the-worlds-most-potentially-disruptive-platform/
7. Insurers rank Amazon as the world's most potentially disruptive platform. https://www.theactuary.com/news/2018/1

1/insurers-rank-amazon-as-the-worlds-most-potentially-disruptive-platform/
8. If You're a Generalist, Advisor, Your Days Are Numbered. The age of the specialist has begun. Advisors who want to grow and succeed from here must differentiate themselves further. By Michael E. Kitces. December 13, 2013. ThinkAdvisor. https://thinkadvisor.com/2013/12/13/if-youre-a-generalist-advisor-your-days-are-number/
9. Morningstar. https://www.morningstar.com/blog/2018/07/12/invest-advisor/html
10. Customer Loyalty and Retention Primer. The Independent Insurance Agents of Dallas. https://www.iiadallas.org/page/75
11. Future Disruption in Property & Casualty (accessed from Todd / Andy research notes)

Chapter 2: Your Clients Need These Services!

How not to put your clients' assets at risk

Making sure that clients' assets are safe – and protected from potential risk - can be a bit like a juggling act. There are numerous financial-related risks they face. These can include market volatility, inflation, falling interest rates, costly healthcare, untimely death and longevity.

There are also individual parameters that must be considered when devising a financial plan for a client, such as timeframe until retirement (or current needs in retirement), risk tolerance, and both short- and long-term objectives.

Understanding the Pyramid of Risk

Knowing how to retain clients – and ultimately to retain the revenue that they bring into your business – can involve having a good, thorough understanding of both the current and future risks that they may face.

The Financial Planning Pyramid

Estate
Planning

Tax
Planning

Investing

Risk Management

Cash Flow

As time goes on, and once clients get some of their more extreme financial obligations behind them – such as the cost of a child's college education – they may finally have the cash flow or liquidity that is needed to start accelerating their future financial planning.

By looking at the "whole picture" with your clients, you are much more likely to retain them for the long-term, as versus just transacting a one-and-done sale of auto or homeowner's insurance or shares of a mutual fund.

Going forward, the Baby Boomer population will need more help as they plan ahead for retirement and for battling the rising costs of healthcare as they age. The process of planning can provide a buffer to extreme price sensitivity. LIMRA studies support the idea that more consumers are pleased with their purchases – and the provider – when some form of planning process has been utilized.

The need for life insurance continues to grow. According to the Insurance Information Institute's 2018 Industry Overview, revenue from life insurance premiums in the United States grew by more than 19% between 2016 and 2017.[1]

Because risk can come from so many different angles, it can be difficult at best for one single financial advisor to ensure that all the bases are covered. It is also important to keep a close eye on changes in the client's life that could require regular updates in their planning.

Although most advisors want to keep all of their clients' assets under one roof, the reality is that one professional can't be an expert in all financial matters. In fact, being a "jack of all trades" usually means you are a master of none, and this can lead to problems in the future.

The good news is that there's a way for you to take part in solving more client needs with additional offerings, without having to add more work hours to your day.

Having a team of specialists that you can call upon for tax, legal, and advanced insurance planning is a must. Taking this type of team approach is not only good for your clients, but it can also free up much more of your time to focus on what you do best.

Don't Be a Jack of All Trades

Having a little bit of knowledge about a lot of topics might be considered a plus in some situations. But this isn't the case when it comes to protecting the whole gamut of financial needs that your clients have.

So, while you may be able to provide clients with a well-diversified investment portfolio, advise them on their employee benefits, or offer ample coverage on their home and auto, there are situations where you may need to call for the expertise of a specialist.

Many financial advisors regularly call upon CPAs and attorneys to answer more in-depth questions from their clients regarding tax and legal issues.

Often, these professionals are long-standing members of the advisor's team.

So, why do advisors think differently when it comes to getting specialized assistance with their clients' risk management needs?

We know that the answer isn't because clients don't have a need for insurance protection. In fact, just the contrary.

According to LIMRA, roughly 70% of consumers agree they don't have enough coverage.[2]

Likewise, many consumers are also open to purchasing more coverage, but they perceive it to be "too expensive." In addition, they don't know who to turn to for advice on the right type and amount of protection.

So, in many instances, just the simple act of letting clients know you can help them with their insurance coverage could open the door to additional opportunities to serve them.

If there is a need for additional risk management tools and strategies – and clients realize they need to fill in coverage gaps - why aren't more financial advisors placing a higher focus on it?

We see many reasons why most firms do not have an intentional strategy to grow their business in this particular area.

First, many do not feel the "pain" of losing their clients to the competition yet. Rather, these advisors are currently earning nice incomes helping with the more traditional financial and insurance needs of their customers. They are not concerned about areas that are not their field of expertise. Unfortunately, though, this can cause overall business to gently erode, causing some clients to seek this help somewhere else, and their advisor often does not know it is happening.

Second, advisors are oftentimes so busy servicing their current block of business that they become more reactive than proactive with their offerings. They don't have time to add any additional components because it takes too much time. Top performers know there is a better use of their time than mastering the intricate details about other offerings, and taking time to market them.

For instance, starting a life or long term care insurance strategy requires an intentional plan for soliciting new business from existing clients. Many advisors feel going this route can jeopardize their existing, recurring revenue streams.

The third reason for not adding new avenues of business is because the staff is busy working on the advisor's existing business. So, many advisors feel that they don't have the time – or the expertise – for proactively soliciting their clients for insurance opportunities.

Another reason is we hear many advisors say they do not want to be perceived as an insurance salesperson. There are some professionals who feel their clients may look at them differently if they try to sell them insurance. They do not want to take the risk that a client who sees them as an objective advisor could do anything that their client could perceive would be salesy.

There is also a prevailing mindset with many wealth managers and traditional multi-line professionals that they do not want to be forced into offering something that they know little about. There can be a natural concern that if they get involved in an area that is not their core competency that they might end up looking like they do not know what they are talking about. They simply do not want to do anything that could put their reputation or professionalism at risk with their clients.

Similarly, many firms just don't have the existing staff or resources to be effective in offering such services competently to their customers. In fact, in many such firms, there is a "scarcity of resources" in order to help with this need, so it is easier not to make it a priority. By taking them out of what they do best, they increase the risks of errors or distracting them away from what is the best use of their time and expertise.

Maintaining and Enhancing Your Fiduciary Status

Over the past several years, the financial services industry has also placed a significant focus on the importance of advisors working in a fiduciary capacity. Fiduciary relationships are all about trust.

You must act in the best interest of your clients. This includes acting with the highest degree of loyalty and care when fulfilling duties – and being personally liable if you do not.

By referring to yourself as a financial planner, then, it is imperative to understand that risk management is part of a good overall financial plan for most of your clients.

Likewise, risk management should be included as a component of wealth management.

Managing risk is designed to protect families in the event of an unforeseen circumstance, such as:

- Premature loss of life
- Protection of assets from an extended health or long-term care need
- Loss of income
- Proper – and cost effective - asset transfer from one generation to the next
- Transfer of a business to ensure continuity, or the sale of a business at an agreeable price

Increased Revenue Per Client Relationship

Increasing your business revenue can entail bringing in more clients, offering additional services to your existing clients, or a combination of both. Of these methods, engaging in more business with current clients is oftentimes the better, faster, and most cost-effective route to take.

On average, businesses spend just 21% of their marketing budget on existing clients, even though this group makes up more than 60% of revenue.[3] One of the primary needs of the future-based advisor, then, is maximizing revenue from current clients.

There are a couple of ways that you can accomplish this. These include:

1. Increasing the average transaction size
2. Increasing the frequency of transactions per customer
3. Focusing primarily on clients who bring in higher revenue

Many financial advisors segment clients based on profitability. That way, in following the "80/20 rule," you can spend more time working with the "A" clients who bring you the most income, and place "B" clients further down the list.

But what if you instead segmented your clients based upon potential needs that they have? As an example, are there clients who have a meaningful insurance need that could move them from the B list to your A list?

When you look at all the needs your clients could have, it's likely that you can grow your clientele organically. If you are successful in making this transition, it can serve your clients better, increase your revenue per client, and increase your bottom line.

Yes, looking at all the needs of your clients can certainly take time. But that time doesn't have to be yours.

This is something that could be outsourced to an individual or firm that specializes in insurance based solutions and strategies. In this case, you can still be involved in the overall process, but without having to take the time to learn all of the intricate ins and outs of advanced insurance planning.

This type of "team" work is exemplified in other industries every day. For instance, most people will see an internist or family practice professional for their annual medical check-up. But if an individual needs more specialized care, such as foot surgery, it's likely that they will go to a foot specialist who is referred to them via their primary healthcare doctor. That way, they can receive the specialized care that they require.

They can also get more of their in-depth questions answered because the foot doctor specializes in that particular area and has likely spent many years studying and working in this niche. Throughout the entire process, the internist is still involved, while the patient can receive the customized care services that they require. So, it's essentially a win-win-win for all.

We understand that some financial advisors don't enjoy any aspect of risk management planning. But these advisors know that managing risk is a fundamental foundation to their clients' overall plans.

So, rather than having you or your team work on this aspect of client planning, an alternate option is to delegate the entire process to an insurance professional and let them manage the process – from the initial discussion to the final placement of the case. Think of these services like you would the services of a CPA or attorney. It is likely that you refer clients to them, based on the unique service they can provide.

How exactly do you frame the conversation with clients to introduce a specialist?

There are several concepts that you want to communicate as you facilitate an introduction, such as letting the client know that:

- The specialist is a part of your team of advisors
- Referring the client to the specialist is in the best interest of the client
- The specialist is competent, objective, thorough, and trustworthy
- The specialist will not make a recommendation that you have not approved first

Getting the process started is easy when using a viable system. We suggest you let the client know what they can expect from start to finish. For instance, the process we use involves the following components:

- Reviewing insurance coverages in order to get an overview of the client's situation
- Going through a needs analysis to evaluate their current situation and see if there are other needs
- Determining whether the client should remain on their current course, or if it would be more beneficial to make some adjustments to their coverage

We think you may be pleasantly surprised to see how a relationship with a specialist in insurance-based solutions could improve the service to your clients and be a good representation of your firm.

Sources

1. Facts + Statistics: Industry overview. Insurance Information Institute. https://www.iii.org/facts-statistics-industry-overview
2. Do You Have Enough Life Insurance? By Kimberly Palmer, Staff Writer. U.S. News and World Report. https://money.usnews.com/money/personal-finance/articles/2014/07/16/do-you-have-enough-life-insurance
3. https://entrepreneur.com/article/300221

Chapter 3: Building a Fence Around Your Clients

How to keep your competitors out

Have you ever had a client tell you that they just purchased an insurance product solution from an advisor down the street because they didn't know you offered the same solution?

Unfortunately, this scenario plays out more often than you might think – even when an advisor has a good relationship with his or her clients. By not bringing up the topic of risk management with your clients, though, it is likely that someone else will. That can open the door to losing clients and losing recurring revenue.

In fact, once clients realize that they have a financial or insurance need that you, their advisor, did not address, one of several scenarios will usually play out. One outcome is that the client will purchase coverage from a different advisor, and that's the end of it. In other words, the client will stick with you for their other financial needs.

But another possible scenario is that, once the other advisor gets their foot in the door, they may start making other recommendations to your client. In that situation, you could end up losing future business from the client. This can put you on the defensive to protect what you've already done – as well as what you *could have done* – for them.

In either case, though, the seed has been sown for potential future competition or potential unrest that may cause the client to trust you less as their advisor. They may even seek a second opinion before moving forward with future recommendations from you. By being aware of their potential insurance needs, you may avoid this scenario and keep it from happening.

The irony here is that as a financial or multi-line advisor, your goal is oftentimes to protect the assets your clients have built over many years. By not covering all their potential needs, *your* business can become more vulnerable to competitors.

So, rather than have clients get these needs filled by a competitor – and risk losing them altogether – it makes sense to provide your clients with viable risk management strategies...even if this area of planning is not your area of expertise.

In many cases, even if an individual or couple knows they have certain needs, they don't always know who they can turn to. Therein lies the importance of letting your clients know you can still help them by calling on your team members who specialize in the area of risk management.

Research has shown that clients prefer to get these risk management services from someone they already trust and with whom they have built a solid relationship. The facts are they already know and trust you, and most would rather work with you, or your firm, on this issue.[1]

Great advisors do not want to leave anything to chance. Rather, they want to control the environment to get the most predictable outcome possible. But, by allowing other advisors who are not on their team to meet with their clients, a negative variable is entered into the equation.

On the other hand, if the risk management specialist is part of a coordinated effort and is representing the advisor's team, the advisor can make sure that the insurance recommendation is consistent with the overall strategy for their client. Going this route can also help to keep the client from seeking advice elsewhere. In addition, it allows you to approve the recommendation to make sure it is consistent with the overall strategy you have working to implement with your clients.

Interestingly, an IIBA study revealed that 70% of customers are open to purchasing their life insurance from their property and casualty provider. Further, 44% of households say that they have some coverage, but need more life insurance.

Who exactly are these people? They can include:

- Your current customers and clients – 3 in 4 already have some insurance and are seeking additional coverage.
- First-time buyers – 1 in 4 currently have no life insurance coverage at all, and 74% of these potential first-time buyers do not have a personal life insurance agent, broker, or financial planner.
- Young and middle-aged households – especially those with children.[2]

So, if you aren't offering coverage to these individuals, *who is*?

Many consumers admit that they don't know who to trust with their protection needs.

Given that, if most of your clients know in the back of their minds that there is a need, where will they feel comfortable getting the advice they need?

The most obvious choice would be you. So, since they already trust you as their primary advisor – then maybe you should have a way to help solve these needs. If you do not have the time, desire, or expertise to do this, it might make sense to outsource it to a professional that you have screened. This way, you can work in conjunction with the insurance professional, and even see their recommendations, before they are discussed with the clients. This can ensure that it is consistent with your philosophy.

Are You Really Covering All of Your Client's Needs?

How exactly can you stay ahead of the competition and ensure that your clients don't move on to seemingly greener pastures, without having to be an expert in a long list of insurance and financial tools?

One way is to make certain that your clients feel comfortable and confident with your recommendations. That comes from providing your clients with the best possible solutions by collaborating with external expert team members who can address in-depth questions and concerns and customize a plan for your clients' specific needs. By outsourcing this to someone you trust will represent your team well, you do not have the constant overhead of funding a position on your staff for someone who may only be needed occasionally.

But where can you find these "team members" that can offer solutions that are aligned philosophically with your firm?

We all want to avoid running the risk of a stereotypical insurance agent giving a sales pitch for a product like permanent life insurance and positioning it as the ideal "Swiss Army Knife" of financial solutions that can solve all the client's needs. Many of us have seen sensational offers that appear to solve all their needs in one plan including:

- Dying too soon
- Planning for college expenses
- Paying for a wedding
- Paying off their home mortgage early
- Providing tax-free income in retirement

Turning "Clunky" Risk Management into a Profitable Client Retention Strategy

In today's fee-based financial services industry, many advisors are moving away from commissions to planning and money management fees. Because the economic engine that drives your business can oftentimes be the fees, human nature tells us that we should spend time on what creates income for our families and our lifestyle. Consequently, many fee-based advisors have very little activity in the risk management space.

There are many advisors who also don't enjoy risk management planning. They feel that this area can be confusing and "clunky," as well as an inefficient use of their time, and in some cases, even "painful" to pursue.

But these same advisors also know that risk management is a fundamental foundation to their client's overall financial plans. By not addressing it, they can leave the door open for competitors to come in and infiltrate their client base.

One of the best ways to prevent this from happening is not to leave yourself exposed such that your competitors have a point of entry. Once a competitor gets in – even if they start by only selling one small policy to your clients – it becomes easier for them to gradually try undermining the work that you have been doing for them.

In other cases, you may not believe that your clients have the need for risk management at all. For instance, you may think, some of your clients have the wealth to self-insure their potential risks. But the truth is that you may actually be putting the client directly in the path of significant financial risk.

Opportunities for Risk Management in Your Business

In a world where competition for clients is fierce, what is it that makes some financial advisors stand out while others seem to fade into the background?

Relationships. Relationships of trust make advisors stand out. Clients trust you to create a financial plan to ensure they don't outlive their life savings. As a multi-line advisor, they trust you to protect the liabilities of the family and their business. YOUR CLIENTS TRUST YOU!

By inference, your clients will most likely also trust someone you refer them to for specialized work.

There will be seasons for the various types of work which may fall into the categories of:

- Inflation protection
- Risk management for their business and family
- Estate Planning
- Protecting Assets
- Planning for longevity risk

Let's take an example of an extended health care event.

The cost of a lengthy struggle with Alzheimer's could completely wipe out a portfolio of $500,000 or even $1 million…and it could do so within a relatively short period of time.

According to Genworth's Cost of Care Survey, just one month in a semi-private room in a nursing home facility averaged more than $7,440 in 2018. This equates to over $89,200 per year. But that's just an average. For instance, some areas, such as Dallas, Texas, fall somewhat below the average at $5,064 per month, while those in South Georgia can anticipate a cost of nearly $7,200 per month for a semi-private room.[3]

Just this one risk could cause clients to lose a lifetime of savings. A reasonable question for us to ask ourselves is:

"How long could your clients sustain a long-term care need before it depletes their assets, as well as your assets under management?"

While completely avoiding a long-term care need is not possible, making sure that clients are prepared for it financially is. They may be perceived as salesy. This can be much more seamlessly accomplished by having the right risk management tools in place.

In many cases, even if an individual or couple knows they have certain needs, they don't always know who they can turn to. That's why it's important that you let clients know you can still help them by calling on your team members who specialize in the area of risk management.

As risk management specialists, we know that many people can take just a small percentage of their wealth and use it to leverage the protection they need to help protect the rest of their portfolio.

We also know how to make risk management cost-effective and flexible, based on your clients' needs.

Many of your mass-affluent, or high net-worth, clients think they have enough money to self-insure this risk. This may be true. You may have even advised some of them to do this.

What many people do not know, however, is that there are ways to use insurance programs to leverage wealth in a more dynamic way to self-insure.

There are now viable options for the old style long-term care insurance that either you "use it or lose it," meaning the insurance premium is an expense that is never recouped if they do not make a claim.

Also, some old-style, health insurance chassis solutions had significant rate increases over the past few years. This can become a financial burden as clients age, particularly if they are on a fixed income. Sometimes it gets so expensive that they end up having to drop the coverage they had paid into for many years.

For example, purchasing an expensive stand-alone long-term care insurance policy could cause clients to lose all of their paid-in premiums if they never have a need for the benefits. But, in today's world, there are other options available for covering a potential need for long-term care. Even seasoned multi-line agents and financial advisors may not be aware of these because it is not their primary field of expertise. That's why we work alongside you, guiding your clients to the solutions that work best for them and their unique situations.

In addition, working with a risk management specialist offers you and your client's options that span far beyond just the basics – because in today's financial environment, basic risk management, or avoiding it entirely, won't cut it.

Some of your clients may have purchased insurance many years ago, but they have not heard from the person who sold them the policy (or policies) since the coverage was initially purchased. Asking the right questions can help to determine whether or not this coverage is still suitable for the clients' current needs. And if not, what adjustments need to be made?

As their trusted advisor, have you considered asking these types of questions to your profile? While it may not be an area you are comfortable advising, or it may not be the best use of your time or your expertise, it could open the door to needs your clients did not know they had.

Working together, as part of your team, a specialist can assist you with making this a routine part of your business, taking inventory of all policies and reviewing them. This could help in determining whether or not their existing policies are still needed. Together you and the specialist can take the necessary steps in designing a more suitable risk protection strategy.

Are Your Clients' Current Plans Setting Them Up for a Future Financial Struggle?

Even if a client has the appropriate amount of risk management coverage, the low interest rate environment of late has negatively impacted the cash value on many permanent life insurance policies.

This may mean that even though they did good planning and execution at the time of taking out the policies, the client may not be on track to solve their potential problems today. It can be an eye-opening experience to do a policy review and let someone know their current plans are not projected to be in force at the age of their anticipated life expectancy.

What risk management strategies are you currently incorporating with your clients? Are you doing any work to protect your clients from the risk of living too long? And if you don't keep your clients' needs protected, does it concern you that others may?

Why You Should Offer the Services Your Clients Need

In most cases, clients will have four identifiable risks or needs for financial protection. These include:

- Income Protection
- Asset Protection
- Protection for Survivors
- Planning for Longevity

Identifiable Risk Quadrant

Income Protection	Asset Protection
If your client cannot work because of an injury or sickness, how long could their family survive financially?	How would an extended healthcare event change the financial plan you create and manage for your clients?
Protection for Survivors How would a premature death negatively affect a client's financial plan if the breadwinner(s) are not here to continue earning income?	**Planning for Longevity** If your client lives longer than the financial plan assumes, how will that affect the spouse's income and the overall financial plan in the future?

Each of these risks can be evaluated by a risk management professional. If it is determined there is a potential problem, sometimes this can be solved by implementing a strategy that takes a small percentage of a client's assets and uses that to protect the rest. And, while discussing risks and constructing the appropriate strategy can admittedly be time-intensive, the time that is used for fact finding and crunching numbers doesn't have to be *yours*.

By partnering with a risk management specialist who is viewed as an extension of your team, your clients – and you – can benefit immensely.

Including a risk management specialist on your "roster," clients can feel comfortable knowing that their most in-depth questions and concerns can be answered, and that their protection is properly aligned with their overall financial plan.

Another reason to consider including risk management offerings to your clients is to minimize your own risk as a business. In fact, not only can you face the loss of clients by not addressing all of their needs, there could be other pitfalls, too.

As an example, advisors could be sued when a client dies without life insurance or goes into a costly nursing home without long-term care coverage but was not offered a policy from a company that promoted itself as providing a full line of protection.[4]

Do Your Clients *Really* Need More Life Insurance?

LIMRA research tells us that the average individual will make seven life insurance purchases throughout their lifetime.[5] But industry research also indicates that multi-line agents only sell a client life insurance twice during the customer's life.

This means that you could be missing *five opportunities* to protect existing clients with this coverage, and to keep your clients from going somewhere else to purchase it. If clients do buy life insurance from another source, it is often because they just simply did not know that their current advisor offered this coverage, or they were not asked to buy.

Why do many of your clients need life insurance?

According to LIMRA, 41% of life insurance shoppers are most influenced to shop for coverage by life events that create the need for protection, such as:

- A change in marital status
- Having or adopting a child
- Purchasing a home

- Receiving substantial assets (such as an inheritance)
- Experiencing the death of a relative or close friend[6]

However, because many consumers do not initiate the process of securing risk based solutions on their own, it is important for advisors to reach out to them. Based on LIMRA studies, a quarter of life insurance shoppers consider this coverage because a sales rep or financial advisor reached out and suggested the protection.[7]

That advisor could be you – but if it's not, who will it be?

The upside to offering life insurance to current clients is that there is the potential for increasing your firm's revenue by approximately 10 to 30%. On top of that, doing so can also increase your client retention.

Just to put this more into perspective, a 1% increase in multi-line agency retention is estimated to be a $40,000 per year increase in revenue for an average sized firm that brings in roughly $500,000 in revenue.

Are You Using the Right Risk Management Strategy with Your Clients…and with Yourself?

While you may or may not be a believer in life insurance, the reality is that this type of coverage has a distinct place in the overall financial planning process. Even clients who already carry life insurance are oftentimes woefully underinsured and policies may be structured to expire prior to their covered need going away.

LIMRA research projects life insurance sales to increase by about 3% per year for the near future. With an aging traditional field force, this means that there is a growing opportunity to serve clients through risk management planning with advisors who have not traditionally offered such solutions to their clients.

For instance, consider our low interest rate environment, where it can take $1 million or more just to generate – or replace - $10,000 or $20,000 in annual income if they are in traditional safe money alternatives. Most professionals are now using a number less than 4% to calculate having enough assets so that clients do not spend down their capital while they still need it.

Are your clients prepared to live on $40,000 per year? Can your clients' survivors live on that amount of income when the inevitable occurs?

With the right risk management plan in place, your clients will be in a much better position to weather any type of financial storm without having to change their lifestyle – or their lives - in the event of the unexpected.

So, if your clients don't implement this strategy through you, who will they turn to? Your clients need a well-executed risk management plan. By not addressing these needs, your clients may be exposed to solutions that do not fit well with the plan you have implemented for them.

If there is no plan in place to transfer the risk of loss of income, your clients could end up having their largest financial storm in the fourth quarter of their life when they may not have the time or the health to recover. Lastly, you need to consider if you want the risk of losing them by asking a competitor about it.

Sources

1. Page 26 of the "to Shop or not to Shop" study – under the heading "Relationship with Sales Rep or FA"
2. Trillion Dollar Baby. The Sales Potential of the Underserved Life Market. LIMRA International
3. Genworth Cost of Care Survey 2018. https://www.genworth.com/aging-and-you/finances/cost-of-care.html
4. Help clients face up to long-term care. By Charles Paikert. June 26, 2018. Accessed Sept. 4, 2019. Financial Planning magazine. https://financial-planning.com/news/long-term-care-issues-facing-financial-advisors
5. To Shop or Not to Shop for Life Insurance. Turning Shoppers into Buyers. By Cheryl D. Retzloff, ACS, LLIF. LIMRA
6. To Shop or Not to Shop for Life Insurance. Turning Shoppers into Buyers. By Cheryl D. Retzloff, ACS, LLIF. LIMRA
7. To Shop or Not to Shop for Life Insurance. Turning Shoppers into Buyers. By Cheryl D. Retzloff, ACS, LLIF. LIMRA

Chapter 4: Staying in Your Own Lane

Focusing on the highest and best use of your time

How much would you pay for advice that would not only increase your income and revenue generation, but would also allow you to focus on what you do best and earn more while working less?

Andrew Carnegie paid $10,000 back in 1890!

As the story goes, Carnegie was attending a cocktail party where he was introduced to Frederick Taylor, a gentleman who was an expert on organizing work. When Carnegie challenged Taylor to tell him something about management that would be "worth hearing," Taylor advised him to "make a list of the ten most important things you can do. And then, start doing number one."

A week later, Taylor received a check for $10,000.

Even though $10,000 was a great deal of money back in 1890, Carnegie felt that Taylor's advice was well worth it – not so much for the items on the list, but rather for constructing it – which forced Carnegie to reflect on his ultimate purpose and in turn, to devise ways to achieve it.[1]

When you start your workday, do you begin with a highly focused plan of action, with the most important items at the top of the list? Or do you instead spend the bulk of your days putting out fires and responding to "urgent" requests?

In other words, are you achieving the highest and best use of your time?

If not, you should be, because doing so can translate into positive benefits for both you and your clients.

Are You Using Your Time for Its Highest and Best Possible Use?

Another 5.3 hours per week are spent preparing for such meetings, with an additional 6.6 hours per week spent doing the supporting financial planning, investment, and other analytical work to answer client questions (either in advance of meetings, or in response to client inquiries that come in via email or telephone). In total, the average advisor spends just short of 27 hours per week on these "direct" client activities.

The next most time-consuming task for advisors is attracting and securing new clients. This, on average, takes roughly 9 hours per week, inclusive of both marketing and advertising, as well as actually meeting with prospects.

Overall, the average financial advisor* reports that they spend 53 hours per week working. When breaking down the tasks of what they do, the most important of these is, not surprisingly, meeting with current clients. But this only occurs, on average, for 8.8 hours per week.

From there, the average advisor spends an average of 5 ½ hours every week on research-related activities to determine the most appropriate financial and insurance tools for meeting their needs and objectives.

The remaining hours of the week are used for the following:

- Administrative tasks (4.2 hours, on average)
- Professional development (3.2 hours)
- Management and other responsibilities (just under 5 hours per week)[2]

When taking a closer look at the breakdown of how lead financial advisors spend their week, it reveals that only about 50% of the typical advisor's working hours are actually spent on client-related activities.

Less than 20% of a typical lead advisor's time is spent meeting with clients.

But is this the best and most productive use of your time?

If you're not currently making the highest and best possible use of your time, it is important to stop and ask yourself why not? And then ask how you can better leverage your time so that you can solve clients' needs (and possibly even uncover additional needs) in the same amount of time…or even less.

Right now is the most important moment of your life. That's because here and now is the only place in which you can act toward achieving the highest and best use of your time going forward. And when you do so, the results you achieve for yourself and your business – as well as for your clients - can be profound.

As you choose to spend most of your time working on important, but non-urgent, tasks, you will also start to feel a renewed sense of calm and control, as you will be better able to focus on providing clients with the full gamut of services they need, as versus just some of them.

*In a "lead" position of being directly responsible for managing client relationships and developing new ones.

Highest and Best Use Defined

As it pertains to time, the "highest and best use" is defined as "the reasonably probable and legal use of one's talent that is physically possible, appropriately supported, and financially feasible, and that results in the highest value for the enterprise."[3]

Achieving the highest and best use of your time requires focusing on what you do best and delegating the rest to someone else. You can leverage your time and expertise by delegating other demands on your time to someone who focuses on the other results you're working to achieve (and who is also keyed in on achieving the highest and best use of their time, too).

Most of your best clients are accustomed to, and like, using different specialists in their life. When properly implemented, this team-oriented approach — where all of the members work together by adding their specialty and expertise into the mix — can produce impressive results. It can also help you to remain laser focused on what you do best with clarity and confidence.

How to Properly Solve Clients' Needs without Spending "Too Much" Time

If you are honest with yourself, many traditional insurance needs are not a high priority for many professionals in the financial services industry. It can be slow. The process can easily take 6 to 8 weeks, and if you don't do it regularly, the process can be excruciatingly painful. But the problem with not addressing the issue is, if your clients have an unforeseen incident and they have not planned for it, it can derail the plan and be devastating to them financially.

Even if you don't bring up the topic, it is possible that you will be asked by clients to comment or provide guidance on their current or considered coverage. The direction that the client goes in with their coverage can literally impact their life, as well as the lives of their loved ones, possibly for many years to come.

But if this is not your area of focus, where should you begin if a client needs your guidance? What should you do? Who can you ask for help?

Unfortunately, some advisors deflect the conversation away from these topics – not because there isn't a client need (because there oftentimes is), but rather because they risk making amateurish mistakes and in turn, losing credibility. This is where having a system in place, as well as an expert to turn to, can be priceless.

Even with the most basic of tasks, having a system in place can be beneficial. For instance, we've all been to the grocery store and most likely had one of the following experiences:

One, you make a list with 10 items to purchase so you can make a dessert for your dinner guests. You go to the store, pick items up one by one, and cross them off your list. You then go home and begin baking the dessert and all goes as planned.

Or, two, you have made the dessert a few times in the past, and you are familiar with what all goes in it. You believe you remember the recipe and know everything you need to buy. As you shop, you purchase everything you *think* you need, and you go home. Later that evening, you begin baking the dessert and you realize you don't have any vanilla extract. So, you note to yourself to make a checklist next time you go to the store!

Many advisors who do not routinely work with insurance-based solutions can often fall into one of the above scenarios when asked by their clients about this type of coverage. In this case, they either follow a system or a checklist, or they move forward thinking that constructing the right life insurance plan is "just like riding a bike – you never forget." But unfortunately, they end up leaving out important ingredients, and the client ends up with a half-baked dessert.

Unfortunately, this "solution" that is put in place can actually end up causing even more problems down the road, such as:

- Mistakes in the beneficiary designations
- Improper ownership of the policy
- Use of the wrong insurance carrier for the client's need

When this occurs, the next time a client asks the advisor about insurance questions, the conversation is quickly changed. The end result is that the client either purchases the coverage they need from someone else (which can ultimately lead to a loss of assets under management for the original advisor). Or, the client's needs go unsolved, essentially leading to financial hardship for the client or their loved ones because of an incomplete financial plan.

How to Uncover Bigger Clients Needs and Provide Thorough Solutions

Shying away from a discussion about life insurance could prevent you from opening your door to new clients, as well as keeping it open for the clients you currently serve.

The very same clients that seek your advice for commercial insurance coverage or investments could also be your best prospects for employee benefits, retirement plans, key employee insurance, and your business continuation planning to ensure there is a successful transfer of their company and their wealth.

Often, working with a specialist can also uncover bigger needs than a generalist can find on their own – and when this occurs, there is usually a more sophisticated solution that a multi-line agent or investment advisor may not be comfortable constructing and implementing on their own.

Staying Focused on What You Do Best

Oftentimes, advisors feel the need to wear several different "hats" so that they can serve as many of their clients' needs as possible, and in turn, keep their clients from seeking advice or solutions from a competitor.

Unfortunately, though, this can sometimes backfire, resulting in incomplete, or even incorrect, solutions being implemented. Wherever you feel obligation, but yet also feel resistance, you are likely running into an area that should ideally be delegated to an expert rather than taking it on yourself.

Here is a perfect example of this. Recently, Andy met with a highly skilled surgeon at the request of his employee benefits specialist. When Andy started handling the paperwork himself, the surgeon commented, "Andy, it bothers me to see someone of your skill set and success handling this yourself. I am surprised you are not focused on the highest and best use of your time."

While this doctor was certainly capable of performing operations from start to finish, he instead worked as part of a team in an effort to provide top-notch services to more patients. In fact, this surgeon was so skilled at what he did -

and had such a high regard for his own time - that he had another doctor open and close the patient while he performed only his specific technique that made him well-known and wealthy. By simply doing this, he was able to increase the number of surgeries he performed every day.

We often meet multi-line insurance or financial advisors whose offerings are like a Swiss army knife. Not wanting to leave anything out, these advisors may make bold claims about solving every possible investment or coverage-related need.

But when you are a hammer, you can start to see life as a nail, and in turn try solving every need with only your "solutions." One thing is for sure, though. There is no one-size-fits-all solution for every client.

Unfortunately, going this route can turn into a market conduct nightmare if you don't perform due diligence and provide proper disclosure. On top of that, we have seen peers lose clients altogether, as well as their professional credibility, when trying to be all things to all clients, rather than reaching out to a specialist.

So, why lose time creating additional work for yourself when you can easily delegate the legwork to a team member who specializes in in-depth risk management strategies?

Achieving the highest and best use of your time does not mean that you, personally have to handle every task that is necessary for attaining results. In fact, in most cases, it means just the opposite.

The doctor's high-level employee benefits specialist we partnered with commented that bringing in a specialist as part of his team enhanced his credibility because he – and his client – knew that the transaction would be done right.

The client commented that he appreciated the advisor was professional enough to admit that he did not have all the answers. The client was also flattered he warranted his primary advisor bringing in a specialist to help with his specific situation. It showed that he understood the highest and best use of time for all of the parties involved, including his client.

If you were to make a list of 10 top-priority items – and then begin working on them – what would these items be?

Sources

1. 816 New York. https://816nyc.com/business-advice-andrew-carnegie-ignore/#.XW_IpW5FxPZ
2. https://www.kitces.com/blog/how-do-financial-advisors-spend-time-research-study-productivity-capacity-efficiency/
3. chiefexecutiveboards.com/briefings/briefing240.htm

Chapter 5: Focusing on Simplicity

Improving simplicity in your life

By nature, financial advice often involves technical language and industry jargon. But, while you need to explain to clients how various strategies and solutions work, it can sometimes be difficult for them to understand.

According to a 2017 Age Wave study on financial and retirement planning challenges, 65% of Americans over the age of 25 believe that the language of finance is confusing or not user friendly.[1]

Unfortunately, if you're not deeply familiar with certain types of planning, you run the risk of leaving clients puzzled. This can lead to frustration, and ultimately to your clients shying away from the use of various financial vehicles. This frustration can undermine the strategy you're presenting when it is something that your clients truly need.

Simplifying Your Life as an Advisor

With thousands of financial advisors for clients to choose from, how can you make yourself stand out and offer the comprehensive services to meet their needs, while at the same time keeping things simple?

One way is to not try being all things to all clients. We've already touched on the old saying, "Jack of all trades, master of none." Unfortunately, many financial advisors can fall into this trap, not wanting to see their clients obtain products from other sources. So, they fill their proverbial "shelves" with a myriad of financial solutions, some of which are completely foreign to them. But is that really the way to provide your clients with the best service?

As a financial professional, it is likely that you are more skilled in certain areas of planning than in other areas. But that doesn't mean that your clients' needs in those other areas should be overlooked or avoided.

By NOT bringing up topics like risk management, you could actually be doing your clients (and their loved ones) a disservice. You also don't want to risk having your clients go to other professionals for solutions and services that you could provide them, but don't.

So, rather than trying to become an expert in a long line of other offerings, or hiring someone full-time who already is, consider how much easier it could be for you to utilize a risk management specialist to assist you on a client-by-client basis.

Going this route can help you to free up a great deal of time that you could otherwise spend searching for answers to client questions about solutions you're not already familiar with. Plus, it will also project a professional, team-oriented approach that your clients will likely be impressed by.

The team approach can allow you to avoid the stress of doing things that are not your core competency while leveraging your time.

Putting yourself in the client's shoes, ask yourself who you would rather work with when implementing and managing your financial plan – a "jack of all trades" or a team of highly skilled specialists?

How the Traditional Advisory Operates

In many firms, there are several different brokerage agencies that advisors are affiliated with. These agencies will oftentimes have different specialties. So, there is the opportunity for the advisor to turn to these agencies in various situations.

Unfortunately, these firms also tend to focus on products, versus customizing solutions that are specifically tailored to fit your clients' needs. In fact, because these firms place more of a focus on products, they tend to "spreadsheet" alternatives and commoditize the process.

But, while this might work well when choosing the right car or computer, it's not necessarily the best situation for clients who are working to grow and protect assets. In addition, going this route can lead to stress and confusion, as the advisor is left to decipher multiple illustrations and multiple options. This can force them to show solutions that might not present well.

Some advisors find themselves caught up in "analysis paralysis" and waste time while second guessing themselves privately.

Likewise, the advisor may not know the finer nuances of what they are presenting. So, this often ends up slowing down the systems and processes that might work well with their core offerings, but not so much with more advanced planning options.

On the contrary, our goal is to create more time for the advisor. This allows you to focus on one relationship between you and your client, while delegating the more in-depth planning details to an expert. This gives you the potential to simplify your life.

Many of the advisors we work with are interested in maximizing the efficiency of the hours they work – primarily because many of them have drawn the "finish line."

A common goal we hear advisors share is they want to try to continue growing their business revenues while having more balance in their personal life.

In this business model, rather than focusing on multiple "product" solutions from a number of different product vendors, you can instead focus on a boutique relationship where the need of the client is "outsourced" to a strategic partner who specializes in risk management.

This can allow you to improve your process by allowing you to do what you do best and delegating the rest. It also lowers your stress level, while typically yielding a better result for both your client and your firm.

As an added benefit, partnering may even allow you to uncover additional client needs. By walking through a full need's analysis, you can bring up areas that should be addressed as part of the overall risk management process.

Yet, there is no such thing as a one-size-fits-all risk management plan. Ensuring financial protection can differ – sometimes substantially – from one client to the next.

Matching up the right protection plan for each individual client can be a tedious and time-consuming project. It also can be risky if your team does not have the time to stay current on the most sophisticated options for your clients.

By partnering with a risk management specialist, you can rely on your team member to do what they do best, while you focus on the day-to-day activities of running your business.

Even if you are involved at every stage in the process, there is no need for you to spend more time completing additional tasks. It also allows you to avoid a need to add any additional staff to your office – or to your payroll.

Taking an Educational versus Salesy Approach

Let's face it, "selling" today simply does not work. A one-sided selling process can create a great deal of tension. Consumers can typically sense a sales pitch and immediately put up their defenses. This can cause them to avoid something they need.

Alternatively, you can position yourself as a trusted advisor who educates customers on the "big picture,". This helps them solve a need. The solutions will not only be beneficial to them, but also to you in terms of client retention and referrals.

Oftentimes, you will be able to position the products and services you offer as the ideal solutions for your clients' needs. You can custom fit these solutions in a consultative manner which allows you to continue building trust with your client. However, as your clients' needs expand – or, as you uncover more of the needs they have – you may have to either provide them with an alternate "solution" or refer them to someone else.

In this situation, that "someone else" can either be a competitor, or they can be a member of your team. Either way, the client has a need and they need to seek a solution. By already having a specialist on your team, even if you're unable to solve such needs, you can point your clients in the right direction and avoid adding another item to your plate that can already be full.

Increasing Income and Client Retention with Less Work

If you are working towards maximizing the potential value of your clients, it is important to create a culture of trust and expertise in your business. The goal of most any associate, firm, or company should be how to do a better job of building existing relationships. These relationships are enhanced when they are based on consultative planning skills that can:

- Build a better relationship
- Increase revenues
- Improve retention

Most multi-line firms will need to begin with training their customer service representatives who talk with clients and prospects on a regular basis.

According to an IIBA study, 70% of customers who work with property and casualty firms admit that they do not know all the product types the firm offers. Most of these individuals admit they are open minded and would be likely to think of their current agent if they needed additional types of coverage. However, most of these consumers say that they have never been asked about other needs by their advisor.

Further, many people will buy life insurance within one year of a major life event, such as getting married or divorced, having children, purchasing a new home, or starting a new business. Who in your business is best equipped to know when these life events take place with clients?

In many cases, it is the customer services representatives (CSRs). A well-trained CSR can look for such opportunities when they are asked to make changes to an insurance plan, such as updating the client's homeowner's policy.

Another way to spot opportunity is at the time a client makes a claim. Typically, people are never more aware of their mortality than when they have experienced a "narrow escape," such as being involved in an auto accident, a house fire, or a burglary. At these times, clients may be interested in talking with someone about protecting their loved ones in case something happens to them.

Respecting You and Your Clients' Boundaries

Using a more consultative approach with your clients – which includes bringing in an expert when needed – you can more seamlessly segue into solving a long list of needs while keeping the "tools" for their financial plan all under one convenient roof.

Going this route can also result in your clients making decisions more quickly, as it is easier for them to see how all the financial vehicles work together. For instance, there is a big difference between the motivation of clients purchasing property and casualty insurance and life insurance.

In this case, many consumers are highly motivated to get their property and casualty coverage in place so they can close on their new house. They are also more motivated to fund a retirement plan or educational plan than they are to plan for life or long term care insurance.

Most people would not dream of driving without auto coverage. Likewise, most would not sleep well at night if they knew they were not covered by homeowner's protection. Therefore, many property and casualty coverage sales are transactional, and are often driven by price.

On the other hand, life insurance is something that many people do not think about until someone asks them some key questions. This is more of an emotion driven process, and coverage is usually purchased for the protection of someone, or something, the client loves.

So, as compared to property and casualty coverage, or funding their investment portfolio, life insurance has an entirely different motivation. Risk management professionals can add additional value to you and your clients' relationships in a way that is easy to understand and relate to for clients.

Partnership Strategies that Create a Win-Win

If you don't feel comfortable bringing up the subject of advanced risk management solutions, you are likely to either avoid discussing these topics, or if you do bring them up, you risk implementing an incorrect – and potentially costly – plan for your clients.

This is where doing joint work with a risk management specialist can be a win for both you and your clients. By sitting on the same side of the table with this professional, your clients can feel that they have a more cohesive plan than having it spread out amongst several different insurance and financial advisors.

Just some of the benefits of doing joint work with a risk management specialist can include:

- **Removal of a dreadful, always changing, and frustrating task.** Many advisors do not enjoy risk management planning strategies. They know that it is a fundamental foundation to their clients' plans. Rather than having you or your team redirect their focus on this, you can simplify your business by delegating the entire process. Someone who specializes in this type of work can manage it from the initial discussion to the final placement of the case.

- **Protection of your client relationships by bringing niche expertise to them.** Think of the risk management specialist like you would a CPA, an attorney, or a money manager. You likely refer your clients to these professionals regularly, based on the unique service they can provide. Like these types of relationships, the risk management specialist won't be *competing* for your client's business, but rather providing *added value* from you as a member of your team. By referring to a risk management specialist, the quality of work will be excellent, and this can help you enjoy a higher quality of life with less stress.

- **Monetization of another aspect of your client relationship.** With many advisors today being compensated via planning and money management fees, rather than commissions, it is important to ensure that your clients' assets are safe, even if the unexpected should occur. That's where a risk management specialist can provide your client and you with a great deal of value.

No solutions are implemented until you approve them. For advisors who do not share in revenue, you can take comfort in knowing your clients are well protected with a plan that compliments what you are building with them.

If you are licensed to offer the solutions that your clients ultimately purchase, you and the specialist can share the revenue.

Sources

1. Finances in Retirement: New Challenges, New Solutions. http://agewave.com/what-we-do/landmark-research-and-consulting/research-studies/finances-in-retirement-new-challenges-new-solutions/)

Chapter 6: Leveraging Expertise

Getting More Accomplished in Less Time

Why is it that only a small percentage of wealth management firms grow faster than the rest of the industry – often despite market and economic volatility?

According to industry consultants, the most successful firms are those that create and promote a team-based service model that serves as the foundation of the organization.[1]

Doing so can provide a win-win for both the client and the business, as each of the professionals on the team can focus on their own individual strengths, and clients receive more in-depth information that pertains to their specific needs. Going this route can also be highly effective from a productivity standpoint, as the business can get more done in less time.

One of the most fundamental strategies for success is leveraging your time and expertise.

Regardless of how successful you are and how many clients you have, there are still only 24 hours in a day. So, by using only your own time, you actually limit your opportunity for results. But if you can leverage other peoples' time – and their expertise - you can increase your productivity and your bottom line significantly.

The 3 Types of Businesses – Which One Defines You?

According to Moss Adams, a century-old research firm that focuses on helping its clients grow, protect, and manage their firms, there are basically three types of businesses. These include the:

- Solo practitioner
- Siloed business model, and
- Ensemble, or true team approach[2]

Let's take a closer look at all of these.

Solo Practitioner

As a solo practitioner, one person is responsible for being the "rainmaker," as well as for covering all of the overhead. The solo practice may have some support staff, such as an administrative assistant. But there are no other professionals.

While a solo practitioner can reap the lion's share of the company's revenue, there are some areas to be mindful of as well. For instance, with a one-person shop, you can run the risk of missing out on business from individuals who question, "What would happen to my money if something happens to you?"

That "something" that clients are concerned about may not necessarily always center on the advisor leaving the business altogether. For example, a solo advisor may not be available for a myriad of reasons, such as illness, vacations, family emergencies, and anything else that could make one person unavailable.

In the past, a vast majority of financial professionals worked with their clients for decades, and then retired with their practice dissipating behind them, and their clients moving on to other advisors.[3]

Solo advisors can also struggle with communicating their expertise in a number of different areas. For example, delivering wealth management services requires knowledge in multiple areas, such as:

- Investments

- Taxes
- Social Security
- Income

It can be difficult to convey to clients that just one person knows all there is to know about all of these different factors. This is where the specialization of a team can be advantageous for both the advisor and the client.

Siloed Business Model

Using a "siloed" business model, multiple advisors work in the same physical office space. In this case, each member of the group shares in the overhead. Yet, while there is some comradery that takes place, in many cases the primary focus of this business model is simply the expense sharing.

Because each of the individuals has a specific focus or expertise, there is little competition in the siloed business model. However, there is also little to no collaboration, so the advisors all have to essentially "eat what they kill."

For instance, in the siloed model, each of the professionals works with their own clients, and to a substantial degree derives income from their own client base. So, where several different professionals may share office space, there is no shared bottom line.

Over time, however, many of the more successful solo and siloed financial advisors have placed a higher focus on nurturing and preserving their existing client base. This strategy can produce more of a reliable and predictable stream of revenue, as it promotes tending to existing client relationships versus jumping from one client and transaction to the next.[4]

Ensemble – The True Team Approach

The third type of business is the team, or ensemble. In this approach, you truly focus on having different people on the team, with each bringing their own unique strengths and expertise. This helps to broaden the services that the business can provide, as well as the value, without the business owner having to take on all of the tasks.

Ensembles also employ different levels of professionals, which combines the enthusiasm, energy, and specialization of various experts. As a result of this leverage, ensembles typically perform better than other types of financial advisory practices. They also tend to:

- Grow faster

- Attract larger client relationships
- Work with higher net worth clients
- Achieve higher levels of profitability, and
- Create long-term value for their principals

In fact, a recent Moss Adams study concluded that mature, ensemble firms generate, on average, twice the income that a mature solo firm generates. According to an AdvisorOne Top Wealth Managers Survey, large firms (exclusively ensembles) have relationships that are seven to eight times larger than the smaller – mostly solo and siloed – firms.[5]

In addition, ensembles also tend to survive the founding generation and pass their knowledge and resources on to the next generation of professionals.[6]

Further, if or when the time comes to sell your financial services business, research has shown that firms with multiple professionals are more valuable as measured by the price paid for a dollar of revenue.[7]

A report from FP Transitions states that the larger ensemble firms generate interest from the large and well-capitalized institutional buyers, such as banks and consolidators, while the smaller siloed practices are typically restricted to smaller buyers with less capital – primarily other financial advisors.[8]

Think about the ensemble approach as you would an orchestra. While each individual musician may be an expert in playing their particular instrument, you get the full effect of the music when they all contribute together to the songs.

In the case of an ensemble approach, you are the conductor, with your primary role being to unify the performers, set the tempo, execute clear preparation, examine performance critically, and shape the ensemble in order to improve future performances – and none of the other experts on your team move forward without your approval.

Similar to an orchestra, much of the conductor's work is not done during the actual performances, but rather in practice and preparation. Part of your preparation may be doing your due diligence on adding future performers to your team who may improve your overall performance.

The beauty of the ensemble approach is that, during the actual time in front of the client, the conductor does not have to be very engaged, because of the ability to delegate this to a certified and highly experienced specialist.

In addition to getting more work done within the same 24 hours each day, by leveraging expertise through an ensemble, you are also enhancing the professional credibility of yourself and your firm.

So, it's not surprising that clients have shown a clear preference for working with ensemble practices.[9]

Is the Ensemble Concept Right for You?

Many financial advisors have a goal of growing their practice. But even in the best of circumstances, one single advisor can only work with so many clients at one time. And, once that limit is reached, there are really only two ways that you can grow your business, and in turn, your income.

First, you could work more hours. But here again, there are only so many hours in a day. Alternatively, you can increase the average size of your client relationships. In other words, uncover more needs and then fill them.

While this method can certainly be challenging, too, it can more easily be accomplished when there are other members of your team who can provide your clients with expert advice and top-notch service.

That being said, we know that not all firms are interested in providing risk management solutions to their clients. Likewise, some financial advisory firms are not looking for a strategic partnership. For these reasons, the ensemble concept is not an ideal fit for everyone.

In other situations, though, there are advisors who see how this concept serves their clients, as well as simplifies their own lives by liberating them from doing time-consuming tasks they don't want to do or are not experienced in doing.

In this scenario, many financial professionals refer to themselves as the coach or the quarterback. They simply outline the strategy while the other team members carry out these tasks.

Before you choose a candidate, it is important that you ensure they can provide your firm with a continuum of both expertise and experience, including:

- **Technical skills and theoretical knowledge.** This describes the specialist's knowledge of risk management theory, as well as knowledge about the tools available for providing solutions to your clients' particular needs.

- **Client relationship skills.** All the knowledge in the world won't matter if the team members you choose do not relate well to your clients. Client relationship skills include the ability to establish and maintain a good rapport, as well as knowing how to explore and uncover needs, and being able to tackle difficult questions and situations. Without good client relationship skills, though, the outcome could be detrimental.
- **Business development skills.** Team members should also ideally be able to work with qualified leads and propose solutions and services, and to ultimately convert prospects into clients.[10]

When partnering with a specialist, there are two different frameworks that you can choose to work within, based on what is best for you and your clients:

Option 1

One option involves having someone work like a traditional wholesaler who provides proposal support, guidance on products, underwriting, and client analysis. You or your staff will perform all the work such as field underwriting, client presentation, completing the application, contacting the client for all questions and necessary forms/requirements, delivering the policy to the client, and ongoing monitoring and servicing of the policy.

Option 2

Alternatively, you introduce your clients to an insurance specialist, and allow the specialist to do what they do best. With this option, the specialist is 100% responsible for the process, and works directly with the clients from the initial discussion to the final placement of the coverage. Basically, the entire process is delegated so that you can spend your time focusing on other things.

Can Your Business Afford Not to Offer Risk Management Strategies?

It is likely that many of your clients fall into this category – particularly if they have loved ones and assets to protect. There are ways that you can meet these protection needs of your clients, without having to spend an inordinate amount of time uncovering coverage "gaps," filling out paperwork, or contacting insurers to track the underwriting process.

According to LIMRA, nearly half of recent life insurance shoppers admit that someone in their household still needs more coverage – and two in ten state that they are very likely to purchase this protection within the next 12 months.[11]

Rather, by introducing such clients to a specialist who handles all of these tasks – without taking you away from your other business and personal obligations – it can provide the leverage that you need to offer the customized solutions your clients deserve.

Sources

1. The Ensemble Practice: A Team-Based Approach to Building a Superior Wealth Management Firm. By Philip Palaveev. 2012
2. Moss Adams Survey of Financial Performance
3. The Ensemble Practice: A Team-Based Approach to Building a Superior Wealth Management Firm. By Philip Palaveev. 2012
4. The Ensemble Practice: A Team-Based Approach to Building a Superior Wealth Management Firm. By Philip Palaveev. 2012
5. 2011 Top Wealth Managers Survey by AdvisorOne, conducted by Fusion Advisor Network
6. The Ensemble Practice: A Team-Based Approach to Building a Superior Wealth Management Firm. By Philip Palaveev. 2012
7. The Ensemble Practice: A Team-Based Approach to Building a Superior Wealth Management Firm. By Philip Palaveev. 2012
8. The Ensemble Practice: A Team-Based Approach to Building a Superior Wealth Management Firm. By Philip Palaveev. 2012
9. The Ensemble Practice: A Team-Based Approach to Building a Superior Wealth Management Firm. By Philip Palaveev. 2012

10. The Ensemble Practice: A Team-Based Approach to Building a Superior Wealth Management Firm. By Philip Palaveev. 2012
11. To Shop or Not to Shop for Life Insurance. Turning Shoppers into Buyers. By Cheryl D. Retzloff, ACS, LLIF. LIMRA

Chapter 7: Next Steps and Case Studies

Where do we go from here?

How many times have you attended a seminar or listened to a motivational business presentation and felt a renewed sense of energy…only to leave your notes on the corner of your desk or in a file drawer for months on end?

It is likely that you learned some beneficial strategies – and that you had every intention to implement them in your business. But then, life got in the way, and you fell back into your day-to-day pattern, thinking that "someday" you would act on what you learned.

It has often been said that knowledge is power. But, knowledge without action is useless. If you are like most people, you may have read this book and thought, "There were some good points in here." We hope you will ask yourself, "How can I implement at least one idea from this book while it is still fresh on my mind?"

Although it's an overused phrase, we all know that the definition of insanity is doing the same thing over again, expecting a different result. So, as you reach the end of this book, one of the decisions for you to contemplate going forward is whether you want to leverage the service and advice model you use with your existing and future clients.

This book was written with a vision for the advisor who is looking ahead and thinking strategically.

Some of you may be pondering questions like, "How does my business need to adapt to change? Are there ways we can serve our clients better while enhancing our professionalism? Should I be focused on the best use of my time? Is it wise to and build a team of strategic partners?"

This model may give you the potential to offer the advantage of true leverage to your clients, as well as the ability to focus on the highest and best use of your time. In addition, it can offer the possibility of enhancing your own professionalism.

For you to pursue this path, though, you need to be willing to make an introduction to a qualified professional who will ensure that the work is done properly, and who will respect your relationship with your clients.

You will need to ask yourself if you think this can truly benefit your clients, while at the same time simplifying your business and your life!

Developing the Right Partnership Strategy for Your Objectives

Many people would agree that a good financial strategist looks for "gaps" in a client's current plan, and then provides advice on how to fill them. This is typically done using various financial and risk management vehicles.

But what about clients who have already adequately covered all their financial bases?

If you're working with a great strategist, they will provide objective advice, and leave the current plan in place.

CASE STUDY

An individual already had two life insurance policies. In this case, a broker introduced a former co-worker to ask our opinion of his existing coverage. The individual had two universal life contracts from a quality carrier.

The first contract had a lifetime death benefit guarantee. On this one, we told him, "This policy is gold-plated. Whatever you do, don't drop this policy." He responded, "I knew I could trust you, and you would not try to sell me something I did not need. But what about this other policy?"

The second policy was a bit different. It was a 20+ year old, current assumption universal life contract with a $250,000 death benefit. Under current premium payments, the policy was projected to expire when the insured reached age 82.

We checked with the carrier, and the policyholder could not pay enough into the policy to get the protected death benefit to maturity. The guaranteed death benefit actually stopped when the insured was in his 70's. Plus, the insured was concerned that the $250,000 of coverage was not enough for him. In addition to that, he was concerned about the lack of a death benefit guarantee because his father, a long-time smoker, died of COPD at age 82.

On top of that, the current policy also had no provision for long-term care coverage. Even though the client had some long-term care coverage through his group benefits at work, he felt that he still needed more.

After analyzing his coverage, and discussing the client's needs and objectives, we came up with a solution for him that included increasing his coverage from $250,000 to $320,000 with a benefit that was guaranteed for life. During the process, we were careful to make sure the client understood there would be new surrender charges. We also let them know the new policy had a commission included that would entail some new charges. After we compared the non-guaranteed contract to the new one, with a new commitment to hold to avoid the surrender charges, it was decided the new plan was a better solution for them.

This solution kept the premium at the same amount that he had already been paying ($325 per month), while at the same time adding a "pool" of $320,000 of long-term care benefits. This pool of long-term care benefits was created by adding a rider to the policy. Should the insured qualify for long-term care benefits under the provisions of the contract, he may access the pool of $320,000 to help pay for long-term care costs. Needless to say, the client was extremely pleased, as was the broker, because our team did 100% of the work after the client was introduced to us.

CASE STUDY

Ensuring Proper Coverage Through Policy Audits

We are frequently asked by advisors to perform life insurance policy audits for their clients. By delegating this otherwise time-consuming task to us, advisors can free up much more of their own time to meet with prospective and existing customers, knowing that risk management needs are being handled professionally.

Recently, an advisor asked for a review of a husband and wife's existing life insurance policies. The husband, age 60, was covered by three policies, and the wife, age 58, had six. After our review with the advisor, we determined the following:

The husband owned two permanent and one term life insurance policy. However, he did not have long-term care insurance coverage. Our recommendation was that he keep the existing term life policy, and "repurpose" the two existing permanent policies into one policy that would provide a death benefit, as well as a long-term care benefit for him.

To facilitate the "repurpose" of the existing policies, we utilized a section 1035 exchange to transfer the old policies to the new one. A 1035 exchange is a provision in the tax code which allows you, as a policyholder, to transfer funds from a life insurance, endowment or annuity to a new policy, without having to pay taxes.

Husband	Cash Value	Death Benefit
Term Policy – Keep	N/A	$403,080
Permanent Policy – Repurpose	$5,116	$50,605
Permanent Policy – Repurpose	$479	$126,055
TOTAL	$5,595	$579,740

We executed the 1035 exchange, and we designed a policy with the same funding structure as his current policies, but it would be paid in full after just 10 years. Then, at age 85, the husband would have a paid-in-full long-term care policy, with a monthly benefit of $6,343. This contract is a linked-benefit plan, which provide for both a small life insurance benefit, as well as an increasing pool of long-term care benefits.

This plan will pay out for a minimum of 6 years, and the "pool" of long-term care coverage will exceed $490,000. As an added benefit, if the husband does not ever use the long-term care benefits, a death benefit will be paid to his beneficiary.

Upon analyzing the wife's five permanent life insurance policies (as well as the one term policy on her), we determined that she had a higher amount of total cash value than her husband. With this cash, we were able to provide her a paid-in-full long-term care policy.

Wife	Cash Value	Death Benefit
Permanent Policy - Repurpose	$14,333	$28,826
Permanent Policy - Repurpose	$17,914	$41,268
Permanent Policy - Repurpose	$13,140	$36,178
Permanent Policy - Repurpose	$10,438	$31,537
Term Policy - Keep	N/A	$541,942
Permanent Policy - Repurpose	$151	$125,000
TOTAL	**$55,975**	**$804,751**

We executed a tax-free 1035 exchange of the wife's cash values, and provided a plan for her that, at age 85, would have a monthly long-term care rider benefit of $5,271, and an overall "pool" of long-term care benefits of $486,795.

One point to note is when a new product solution is acquired, it will include acquisition fees such as sales loads and compensation paid to the agent, and possible surrender charges for a specified period of years. These charges and fees should be reviewed by and disclosed to the client in the customized proposal provided by the selected carrier.

In the case of this couple, the original purpose of the life insurance coverage had been to replace income in the event that one or the other passed away. But now that the clients were older – and didn't need the coverage for income replacement – we were able to repurpose it for asset protection due to an extended healthcare event.

CASE STUDY

In another instance, we worked with an RIA from California and his business owner client. The third-generation family-owned business had an executed buy-sell / stock redemption plan, with life insurance as the chosen funding mechanism that would provide liquidity to their plan.

The existing coverage consisted of term life insurance policies, which were due to expire within the next three months. In this case, there were six policies needed, with the insureds ranging in age from 63 to 70.

As part of our process, we began with field underwriting where we communicated directly with all six of the insureds. In doing so, we learned of their health status, and were then able to provide realistic proposals, along with a range of premiums, based on each of the individuals' health.

After that, we determined the best insurance carriers to apply with, and then moved forward with the application process. In order to move the process along, we also sent cover letters to the insurance companies which introduced them to the applicants and detailed the reason(s) we were requesting the coverage – including the financial insight into the reason we needed it.

The outcome of this case was a total cumulative life insurance benefit of $7 million on the six insureds, with an annual premium of $44,500. This outcome was a much better solution for the family-owned business succession.

Converting Coverage that has an Expiration Date

In many situations, people will purchase term life insurance because it can typically provide a large amount of coverage for a little premium – particularly if the insured is young and in relatively good health at the time of policy application.

However, as its name implies, "term" life insurance will only remain in force for a set amount of time. So, if coverage needs are ongoing, term life insurance coverage could expire while the insured still has a financial need for it.

Today, however, many term insurance policies have an option to convert the policy over to a permanent form of life insurance coverage – often without the need to provide any medical documentation or prove evidence of insurability.

This can be an excellent feature, especially in the event that an insured has a change in health status (which could deem him or her uninsurable) and the term policy is scheduled to expire or even to stay in force, but at a significantly higher premium rate down the road. Because of this, we are frequently asked to analyze the possibilities for clients who are covered with term life insurance.

CASE STUDY

As an example, an advisor had a case where a business had purchased a key executive policy on an employee when the employee was age 51. The policy was issued with a preferred non-smoker rate, and provided 10 years of coverage with a death benefit of $10 million.

Luckily, the plan also had a conversion option. That's because over the next several years, the insured developed some significant health issues that made him uninsurable. However, the company still needed to maintain life insurance coverage on this individual.

Because of the term policy's conversion option, the process of securing longer-term coverage was relatively simple. Here, we executed a conversion application, and were able to obtain $3 million of coverage through a low-cost, minimum funded permanent life insurance plan at preferred non-smoker rates, for a premium of just $21,000.

CASE STUDY

In a similar scenario, a fee-based advisor referred us to a client of his who had purchased a 10-year level term policy with a $500,000 benefit. This policy had an annual premium of $2,730. It also included a conversion option.

We were introduced to this client 10 years and 10 months into the policy's term. He had been diagnosed with terminal cancer, and this $500,000 policy would provide a crucial financial benefit to his wife.

Typically, when a term life insurance policy reaches the end of the level term period, the premiums will increase exponentially if the insured remains in the plan. In this case, in order to continue his policy in Year 11, the original premium of just over $2,700 per year jumped to more than $31,400...and would continue to increase annually afterwards.

However, because of the policy's conversion option, it gave the client the ability to change the plan to one with a levelized premium which in this scenario would be $21,875 for as long as the insured was alive.

The conversion feature provided for a new life insurance policy with a level premium. Plus, the terminally ill client – who could never medically qualify for a new life insurance policy – was able to continue his much-needed coverage for the benefit of his wife.

Planning for Longevity

As a type of risk management solution, annuities can provide ongoing income if an individual ends up living "too long." We are often asked to review annuities, then, to ensure that they are still performing the way clients had anticipated them to, as well as to determine whether or not the annuity is still the right fit for the client's need.

CASE STUDY

On one occasion, we were asked to review an existing qualified variable annuity for a client of a fee-based financial planner in Tennessee. The annuity had a value of $883,740.22, a death benefit of $1,344,406.36, and a net insurance benefit of $460,666.14.

The client liked the fact that the net insurance benefit would be paid out to his beneficiary upon his passing. However, the financial advisor felt that the client had better investment options that could be accessed outside of the variable annuity –

primarily in the investment models that the advisor's firm had available. But, the client did not want to give up the net insurance benefit by moving away from the annuity.

In our analysis of this case, we determined that the annual variable annuity fees were 3.3% per year, or $29,163.43.

Plus, upon the client's death, the net insurance benefit from the annuity would be taxable to the beneficiary at their ordinary income tax rates. This could significantly reduce the net amount of payout to the beneficiary.

Upon further review, we recommended a more tax-efficient and lower-cost strategy, which would still accomplish the client's goal of retaining the net insurance benefit. As a replacement for the taxable insurance benefit (originally $460,666 with the annuity), we recommended an individual life insurance policy with a face amount of $350,000. Because the life insurance policy's death benefit would be received income-tax free to the beneficiary, they would be able to receive the full amount from the policy, without Uncle Sam taking a share of the proceeds. The annual premium on this policy was $10,159.

The client's advisor then recommended that the client transfer the annuity balance to his firm's investment models, which the client did, for a management fee of 0.75% per annum. In summary, we accomplished several items in this case, including:

- Reduction of the client's annual fees by more than $12,300
- Creation of a more tax-efficient wealth transfer strategy by using a traditional life insurance policy (which has an income-tax free death benefit, as opposed to the taxable death benefit from the variable annuity)
- The strategy was effective because the client was insurable at an acceptable health rating. If the client was not medically insurable, using life insurance wouldn't be an option
- A detailed summary of the analysis is shown in the table below

Variable Annuity Analysis

VA Contract Value	$883,740.22	
VA Death Benefit	$1,344,406.36	
VA Net "Insurance"	$460,666.14	
	VA Costs	**Firm Costs**
M&E Fee	1.40%	0.00%
GMIB Rider	0.45%	0.00%
GMDB Rider	0.45%	0.00%
Avg Fund Expense	1.00%	0.75%
Total Costs	**3.30%**	**0.75%**
Expenses in Dollars	$29,163.43	$6,628.05
GUL Premium	$ -	$10,159.00
Total Cost	$29,163.43	$16,787.05
Annual Savings	**$12,376.38**	

CASE STUDY

In another situation, a health insurance broker contacted us to seek our opinion of an existing annuity portfolio for a close friend that he had not done business with previously. The man and his wife had an extensive financial portfolio, and they had many different fixed indexed annuities, as well as multi-year guaranteed annuities (MYGAs). Due to some bad financial choices in the past, this couple was risk-averse, and their primary objective was to obtain a large, guaranteed income in retirement.

Prior to our meeting with the couple, the broker supplied a list of the existing annuities that they owned. We were then able to conduct an in-depth analysis of the performance of the fixed index annuities, as well as the rates on the multi-year guaranteed annuities, and on the credit quality of the insurance carriers that had issued all of the annuities.

We were then able to show the couple which were good companies, and which were good annuity contracts. For example, some of their fixed index annuities were renewing with caps of 4.5%, while the market was at a 6% cap (meaning that the couple was essentially losing out on the potential to earn 1.5% more). Likewise, one of the multi-year guaranteed annuities was renewing at 1.5%, while the market was at closer to 3%.

On top of that, some of the annuities they owned were with an insurance company that had an A.M.

Best rating of B+ (whereas insurers with ratings of A or better are considered to be more financially stable). The couple also had a contract with a small insurer that had other concerns.

We explained to the couple that, while their money was guaranteed, we were concerned about the credit quality of the companies that were making the guarantees.

This also was a concern to the clients as they had a very low tolerance for risk.

Taking into consideration the clients' needs, as well as what was currently available in the market, we were able to do the following for these clients:

- We INCREASED the cap on their fixed index annuity from 4% to 6% (meaning that they had the opportunity to earn an additional 2% if the underlying index performed well)
- We increased the rate on their multi-year guaranteed annuity from 1.5% to 3%
- We placed them into annuities with carriers that had and A+ A.M. Best ratings, as versus the B+ rating of their current carrier

In addition to that, while we had initially met with the clients to discuss a $400,000 contract, we left with transfer paperwork of over $1.2 million – and, less than 60 days later, the clients contacted the broker with another $200,000 for him to deposit into a new contract. The broker looked like a hero to these clients, while our team did 100% of the work.

The broker was so pleased with these results that he introduced us to another couple who had over $865,000 in a fixed index annuity with a cap of 1.5%. We made sure the client understood they were moving money from a contract that was out of surrender to a contract that contained a surrender charge. They understood there were no fees or upfront charges to make the transition. We explained that a surrender period was necessary to compensate their broker, since their broker was not charging a fee and there was no up-front sales charge. Upon careful analysis, it was decided the exchange was better than leaving their money with a company that was limiting their upside potential to 1.5%.

Once the broker connected us with the client, our team got to work!

CASE STUDY

Locking in More Flexible Alternatives for Long-Term Care Coverage

A health insurance broker brought a bill for $7,000 for a traditional long-term care insurance policy by our office. It was for a policy on his 80-year-old father. The original cost of the policy had been $4,000 per year, but now at nearly double that amount, it was causing his father a financial hardship.

In addition, the broker and his father had some additional concerns, including:

- The need to keep this long-term care coverage, as his father's wife already had Alzheimer's disease and they understood the need to keep the coverage, but wanted to know if there was a more affordable alternative, and
- There was no way for the broker's father to recoup any of his paid-in premium if he never filed a claim on the long-term care coverage

We met with the broker and his father, and we discovered that the father had $325,000 in a non-qualified annuity that he had originally purchased for $100,000. The father said that his goal was to leave that money as an inheritance to his family when he passed away. Unfortunately, there were some potential problems with this approach.

One was that the father's heirs would likely inherit an annuity with a low cost basis and end up with large taxable gains. These gains would likely be taxed at ordinary income tax rates, as versus lower capital gains tax rates.

We explored the idea of using $200,000 from the father's annuity to fund a qualified long-term care annuity that was issued by an A+ rated insurer and that focused on annuities that qualify for tax-free distribution of the annuity benefits, based on a little-known provision in the Pension Protection Act of 2010.

Using this strategy, we were able to get an annuity in less than one week that leveraged the father's annuity dollars into a $500,000 "pool" of money that can be used as tax-free long-term care benefits should he have to file a claim.

But, if he never has to make a long-term care claim, the family would receive the original $200,000 back in the form of a non-qualified annuity benefit. In addition, the father was able to get a non-forfeiture option on the original policy for a little more than $40,000 of paid up benefits at no additional premium.

The net result is that we were able to help the 80-year-old father accomplish the following:

- Save over $7,000 per year in cash flow (i.e., the premium on his original long-term care policy)
- Make use of an existing asset that was not being utilized
- Increase the amount of his total coverage
- Retain the asset within his family if he did not make a long-term care benefits claim

We explained to the annuitant that they were likely to get a lower return on the annuity since it had the internal charges for the long-term care coverage. We also made sure the annuitant understood they would start a new surrender period. When he considered the alternative of keeping a plan that was increasing in cost and made no provision to return premiums if he never made a claim, he and his son determined that was a good trade-off.

Our team took care of 100% of the work in this case, and we were able to realign the father's assets, once we knew what his objectives were.

> *After the new plans were in place, both the man and his son stopped by our office to thank us for the job we had done and for their new peace of mind.*

CASE STUDY

Using Needs Analysis to Determine Current and Future Goals

While many clients may have a good idea about how they want their current and future financial picture to look, going a bit deeper with a needs analysis can help to determine the right amount of coverage that an individual or couple should have based on financial needs and/or financial liabilities. We typically use a needs analysis to ensure whether or not current needs are in fact being met, as well as to see if there are any protection "gaps."

We were recently referred to a husband and wife who had high-school age children. Both spouses worked and earned nice incomes. They each also contributed to personal savings plans, and both spouses had existing life and disability insurance through their employer benefit plans.

Their current fee-only financial advisor felt that the couple was not adequately covered, though, in case of the unexpected.

Therefore, we took an inventory of "what they owned and why then owned it."

We then walked through the need's analysis process, which included gathering the following information from them:

- Income needs of the survivor if the other had an untimely death
- Current income from employment, as well as income from other sources (such as rental income from property investments, etc.)
- Amount of income to be replaced, and for how long
- Current monthly expenses and debts
- Future college costs for their children
- Current assets in savings and retirement plans
- Current amount of existing life insurance

After reviewing all of the data, we made the following coverage recommendations:

For the husband, we suggested that he keep his current life insurance coverage through his employer-sponsored benefit plan. In addition, we also recommended that he "ladder" a total of $1,250,000 in additional life insurance coverage via a 15-year term policy with $1 million in coverage, and a 20-year term policy with the other $250,000 benefit. This laddering matched the high-income replacement need when the children were in college, and it would automatically reduce when they no longer had the high cost of tuition to pay.

We also made several recommendations for the wife. These included keeping her current policy in force – which had an additional $500,000 of coverage – for 15 years, and to also secure a new 20-year level term life insurance policy with a benefit of $250,000 (in order to provide liquidity similar to her husband's).

Coverage Needs for Business Owners

While many people use risk protection strategies to ensure that their loved ones are financially protected, there are others who can also benefit from the coverage that life insurance can provide. This includes business owners and partners.

CASE STUDY

A fee-based advisor introduced us to two business partners who currently had a buy-sell agreement in place. However, the agreement lacked a funding mechanism and neither partner had any existing life insurance coverage in place. After we reviewed this agreement – along with the formula included in it should the unexpected occur with one or the other partner – we determined that each of the partners needed $2.3 million in coverage.

In this particular case, one of the business partners had a history of substance abuse. This is considered a significant risk for life insurance carriers. Therefore, we reviewed the medical history with several highly-rated insurance companies, and we presented both partners to two different insurers.

Ultimately, we were able to secure the much-needed coverage for these business partners at a price point that was affordable for them. On the partner with substance abuse, for every few years that he continues to extend his sobriety, the higher premium rating on the policy can be decreased.

So that insureds don't miss out on the opportunity to attain a lower premium, we offer as part of our ongoing service model a notification system that reminds us to review policies in the future so that a better policy rating – and consequently a lower premium – can be obtained.

Getting Off the Starting Blocks

How can you determine whether the services of a risk management specialist are right for you and your business?

The first step is to schedule a time for us to talk and to walk through more of the details of how the process works – and how it can benefit you and specific clients of yours.

Go through your client base and ask yourself if you are working with anyone who fits any (or all) of the following scenarios:

- Someone who has had a 20% increase in income in the past year
- Recently changed jobs in the past six months
- Increased debt or accepted a new financial responsibility
- Professionals, executives, or entrepreneurs who are making maximum contributions to qualified plans

- Have their business or real estate as their largest asset
- Currently receiving Required Minimum Distributions
- Widows or widowers who are trust beneficiaries
- Own cash value life insurance that they have had in force for at least 15 years
- Own non-qualified annuities that are at least ten years old
- Have named a charitable organization as the beneficiary of their IRA
- Business owners with key employees they need to retain
- Own life insurance and have not paid, or do not plan to pay, any additional premiums
- Have had a significant change in health and own life insurance
- Have received notification of premium increases on long-term care insurance policies

If you can think of any clients that fit into these positions, you can most likely bring creative and thoughtful ideas to them – particularly if you work in conjunction with a risk management specialist.

What to Do as Soon as You Close this Book

While the information presented here is still fresh in your mind, it's likely that you have additional questions regarding how the ensemble model can truly benefit you, as well as your business and your clients.

Because all advisors have different objectives, these are questions that can really only be answered on more of a personal basis – and we welcome a one-on-one call or visit with you.

We offer a multitude of specialized services that can protect what is important to your clients, as well as uncover other potential needs, including:

- Policy audits and reviews
- Risk reviews
- Policy inventory study
- Policy conversions
- Re-purpose options
- Guidance with policy loans
- Options for un-needed coverage
- Policy improvement options
- Premium efficiency
- Leverage

We are insurance professionals who have profound respect for the job that you do.

We work with other professionals in a collaborative way to make sure their clients are served well in the risk management stage of good financial planning.

If this book - and its corresponding business strategies - is not a good fit for you and your practice, that's perfectly ok. We know that there is no such thing as a one-size-fits-all strategy, for clients or for advisors. But if it may resonate with one of your colleagues or associates, please feel free to pass it on to them, or let us know and we will send them a copy with your compliments.

We work with employee benefits specialists and multi-line professionals to make sure their key business partners' needs are assessed in business continuing planning, key employee retention, and executive benefits.

If this book has prompted you to move forward and to consider a potential partnership to serve your clients, we encourage you to give us an opportunity to work with you on one opportunity to see how it goes. We work in a confidential manner where your business is never discussed with other professionals.

We also understand that these are *your* customers. So, we never approach your clients with any ideas or concepts that we have not first cleared with you. Last, we will never do work with your clients, after the fact, and fail to let you know. We look forward to hearing from you and working together to enhance your business.

To your success!

Andy Martin, ChFC, CLU and Todd Russell, CFP®, ChFC, CLU

Additional Resources

Where to Find More Information on Growing Your Ensemble

More information about Andy Martin and Providence Partners can be found by visiting: www.providencebenefits.com.

Additional information about Todd Russell and Private Client Strategies can be found at: www.privateclientstrategies.net.

About the Authors

Andrew S. (Andy) Martin, CLU, ChFC

Andrew (Andy) Martin entered the financial services industry immediately upon graduating with honors from Birmingham-Southern College. He spent a total of 32 years at First Protective as a sales manager and a leading producer until being promoted to President – where he served for 19 years.

Under Andy's leadership, First Protective led Protective Life, and ProEquities in sales for all 19 consecutive years. First Protective was generally regarded as the largest financial services marketing firm in the south when Andy took early retirement.

In 2017, Andy purchased an existing agency and renamed it Providence Partners. Providence quickly established itself as a leader in the marketplace by offering SUSTAINABLE GAP to insurance and employee benefits professionals.

Providence Partners specializes in risk management and planning for both businesses and business owners. The professionals at Providence Partners enjoy working with other financial advisors, and they use their expertise to help with providing insurance based solutions to people who do not specialize in working with these concepts.

In addition, Andy is asked frequently to speak within the industry. He has presented at some of the largest insurance industry venues, including the Million Dollar Round Table, the Asia Pacific Life Insurance Conference, and the Grant Taggert Symposium. He has also been published in leading industry publications such as Round the Table, LIMRA Marketfacts, GAMA Journal, and Advisor Today.

Andy is married and has three grown children. He is active in his community, being on the Board of Directors for the Fellowship of Christian Athletes at the University of Alabama, as well as serving as a Board Member at Glenwood, Inc., a non-profit for people with autism.

More information about Andy and Providence Partners can be found by visiting: www.providencebenefits.com.

Todd Russell, CFP, CLU, ChFC

Todd Russell is the Managing Director at Private Client Strategies, LLC. He has a passion for helping advisors and their clients understand the risk their family and businesses can have in the event that they die prematurely, or have a long-term, end of life illness. He frequently stresses that insurance policies are not magical – so owning them in the time of need is a priority!

He began his career in 2002, and quickly became a joint work pioneer. As a 17+ year risk management specialist, Todd approaches the coverage conversation from a position of asking questions, as well as educating advisors and clients.

Todd has earned several insurance industry professional designations, including the CERTIFIED FINANCIAL PLANNER practitioner (CFP), Chartered Life Underwriter (CLU), and Chartered Financial Consultant (ChFC).

In addition to his business experience with life insurance, Todd has also endured personal situations where he has seen first-hand the power of having coverage. Todd's father died after a five-year battle with cancer. But approximately four years prior to his diagnosis, Todd's father purchased a life insurance policy from Todd. In fact, the very first client that Todd paid a death claim on was his Dad.

Todd grew up in a small town outside of Birmingham, Alabama, and spent much of his time in the outdoors playing football, hunting, and fishing. He attended the University of South Alabama, where his met his wife Kari. Todd works and plays hard. He and his family reside in the Greater Nashville, Tennessee area.

You can typically find Todd on the weekends pacing up and down the sidelines of his children's athletic events. He has a unique sense of humor and enjoys making those around him feel special and laugh.

Todd has been a speaker at several of the insurance industry professional conferences throughout the years.

Additional information about Todd can be found at: www.privateclientstrategies.net

Disclosures

The author is a registered representative of Lincoln Financial Securities. Securities and investment advisory services offered through Lincoln Financial Securities Corp., a broker/dealer (member SIPC) and a registered investment advisor.

The material here reflects the views of the author and not necessarily those of Lincoln Financial Securities or its affiliates. This material is intended for educational purposes only and should not be used as investment advice or recommendations.

This book highlights important industry regulations and concepts. Please review these resources and concepts and consult your tax, financial and legal professionals before implementing or making changes in a retirement plan.

Annuities are long-term retirement savings or income vehicles. There are fixed and variable annuities available; variable annuities are sold by prospectus. An investor should carefully consider the investment objectives, risks, charges, and expenses of the variable product and its underlying investment options carefully before investing. The prospectus contains this and other information about the variable product and its underlying investment options. Always read it carefully before investing.

All rights reserved. No part of this book may be used or reproduced in any manner whatsoever without written permission from **the Author** except as provided by the United States of America copyright law or in the case of brief quotations embodied in articles and reviews.

The scanning, uploading and distribution of this book via the Internet or via any other means without the permission of the publisher is illegal and punishable by law.

Please purchase only authorized electronic editions and do not participate in or encourage electronic piracy of copyrighted materials. Your support of the author's rights is sincerely appreciated.

www.ingramcontent.com/pod-product-compliance
Lightning Source LLC
Chambersburg PA
CBHW021414210526
45463CB00001B/358